SIMPLY DELICIOUS
Crock Pot
Cookbook

Recipe selection, design, and book design © Fox Chapel Publishing. Recipes and photographs © G&R Publishing DBA CQ Products, unless otherwise noted.

Shutterstock images: Dychkova Natalya (Verso Folio illustration), (22, 32, 38, 44, 50, 56, 62, 66, 102, 154, top); Elena Veselova (1); Keya (2), (21, 27, 29, 31, 37, 43, 49, 55, 59, 65, 69, 71, 113, 141, fork and spoon illustration), (34), (46, 142); Iryn (5, 6, 80, illustration); Ronald Sumners (8); bsd studio (9, top); TMA Harding (9, bottom); Bernd Schmidt (10); Barnawi M Thahir (11, pan illustration); Jiri Hera (11, bottom left); juliawhite (11, top); Lifestyle Travel Photo (11, bottom center); New Africa (11, bottom right); Angelika Heine (12); sherwood (13); robtek (16, bottom right); FoodAndPhoto (17, bottom); ungvar (17, top); Askhat Gilyakhov (18, 144); AS Foodstudio (22); Tunsale Ismaylove (24); tetiana_u (40, 152); oksanashu (73, bottom); Charles Brutlag (92); cupuuu25 (94); Back one line (104); Sahs (108); suns07butterfly (110, right); Brent Hofacker (112); Irina Rostokina (113, bottom); Yanina Nosova (52, 136, illustration), (118); Simple Line (126, 148, 156).

ISBN 978-1-49710-390-0

Library of Congress Control Number: 2023936991

To learn more about the other great books from Fox Chapel Publishing,
or to find a retailer near you, call toll-free
800-457-9112 or visit us at *www.FoxChapelPublishing.com*.

We are always looking for talented authors. To submit an idea, please send a brief inquiry to acquisitions@foxchapelpublishing.com.

Printed in China
First printing

SIMPLY DELICIOUS
Crock Pot
Cookbook

Anne Schaeffer

Includes Vegetarian Options

Amazing Slow Cooker Recipes for Breakfast, Soups, Stews, Main Dishes, and Desserts

CONTENTS

8 INTRODUCTION

14 SOUPS & STEWS

116 DESSERT

124 MEALS FOR TWO

166 INDEX

Introduction

Ah, the slow cooker. Just as the name implies, it is a vessel of cooking that takes delicious ingredients and slowly cooks them to perfection. The slow cooker is one of the most convenient and hassle-free ways to cook your favorite soups, stews, breads, desserts, and more. All you have to do is prepare your meal components and let your slow cooker take care of the rest—in the morning before work, pop in some ingredients. Throughout the day, your house will slowly fill with the delicious smell of food until finally you come home to dinner ready to be served. What could be better?

If you are a beginner at slow cooking, have no fear. I'll provide some tips and tricks on how to get started. The most popular type of slow cooker is called the Crock Pot. You can find these at almost any kitchen supply store, and even some grocery stores. The recipes in this book will cover all major meals and some mini slow cooker ideas, depending on how many people you plan to cook for. Whether it's the whole family or just you, there's something for everyone within these pages and underneath the lid of your slow cooker of choice. So, shall we get started?

YOUR SLOW COOKER SIZE

	2 qt.	3 qt.	4 qt.	5 qt.	6 qt.	7 qt.	8 qt.
2 qt.		multiply by 1½	multiply by 2	multiply by 2½	multiply by 3	multiply by 3½	multiply by 4
3 qt.	divide by 1½		multiply by 1⅓	multiply by 1⅔	multiply by 2	multiply by 2⅓	multiply by 2⅔
4 qt.	divide by 2	divide by 1⅓		multiply by 1¼	multiply by 1½	multiply by 1¾	multiply by 2
5 qt.	divide by 2½	divide by 1⅔	divide by 1¼		multiply by 1⅕	multiply by 1⅖	multiply by 1⅗
6 qt.	divide by 3	divide by 2	divide by 1½	divide by 1⅕		multiply by 1⅙	multiply by 1⅓
7 qt.	divide by 3½	divide by 2⅓	divide by 1¾	divide by 1⅖	divide by 1⅙		multiply by 1⅐
8 qt.	divide by 4	divide by 2⅔	divide by 2	divide by 1⅗	divide by 1⅓	divide by 1⅐	

RECIPE SLOW COOKER SIZE

Slow cookers come in a variety of different sizes, so make sure you adjust your chosen recipe to your cookware.

YOUR COOKWARE

The most common size of slow cooker is in the 5- to 7-quart range. However, some of these recipes were made and tested in smaller pots, ranging from 1½ to 7 quarts. Don't panic! All recipes can be readjusted to your slow cooker size. All recommended sizes are listed with the recipes, but feel free to use this conversion chart for your convenience.

If you have a half-quart slow cooker, round up to the next whole size. For example, if you are converting a 6-quart recipe to fit your 1½-quart slow cooker, base your measurements off the 2-quart conversion. Also, the multiplications factors are quite specific. In most instances, you can eyeball the math and convert it to your taste.

Always fill your slow cooker halfway with components, but never more than two-thirds full. This is to ensure food quality and safety when cooking. The less full your slow cooker is, the faster it will cook. Also, your slow cooker insert can crack when exposed to sudden temperature changes. If the insert was refrigerated, let it sit at room temperature for 30 minutes before heating it up. After cooking, let it cool down for at least 30 minutes before refrigerating.

Keep in mind that some slow cookers have a "hot spot," so be sure to rotate the insert halfway through cooking if this is the case. Even cooking is very important when using a slow cooker! This also means keeping the lid on for the duration of cooking unless specified otherwise by the recipe. If you remove your lid during cooking, heat can escape, which extends the cooking time by nearly 30 minutes. Also consider that oval cookers tend to hold more quantities and larger pieces of meat, while round cookers are usually best for soups and baked goods.

If you're looking to buy a new slow cooker, its best to consider how many people you'll be cooking for. You can reference this chart when shopping:

Number of People	Crock Pot Size
1 to 3 People	1½ to 3½ quarts
4 to 5 People	3 to 4½ quarts
6 to 8 People	6 to 7 quarts
9 to 10 People	7 to 8 quarts

There are two types of slow cookers on the market: manual and programmable. Some come with both options! Either will work just fine, but manual means you must keep track of your cooking time and know when to change temperatures. Programmable slow cookers will automatically switch temperatures at the time you tell it to. However, never delay starting your cooker after putting ingredients into the pot. This could prevent your food from cooking safely and cause bad bacteria to grow.

When you're serving your food, avoid using metal utensils, which can scratch the surface of your slow cooker insert. Instead, use a wooden or nylon serving spoon. Once you've packed up your leftovers or devoured your dish, immediately rinse your slow cooker insert with hot water, then fill it with hot soapy water. Let it soak for a few minutes before taking a soft sponge to the inside.

KITCHEN ACCESSORIES & MUST-HAVES

Other than your slow cooker, there are appliances and essentials that will be required for most slow cooker recipes. Be sure to stock up on these before you begin cooking!

> Immersion blenders are used in a few soup recipes to puree ingredients.

> Bouillon powder (chicken or vegetable) is needed for some slow cooker recipes for ultimate flavor.

> Skillets are required for many recipes that need pre-browned veggies or meats.

> Stock recipes are provided in the beginning of the book, but feel free to buy your own to save time.

> Spices are the ultimate must-haves when using a Crock Pot! Be sure to review your desired recipes to buy the ones you need. Of course, it's always helpful to have a good variety of spices in the kitchen.

> Cornstarch and flour are required in many soup recipes.

> Oil is used for browning and sautéing ingredients, and for coating your insert for baking recipes.

> Slow cooker liners are convenient if you wish to avoid a mess when you're finished cooking. They're not necessities but are some people's go-to accessory.

FOOD SAFETY

It goes without saying that a good bit of preparation goes into slow cooking. When thinking about prep, keep in mind that most meals require six to nine hours of cooking in the pot. Be sure to fully thaw frozen meats and vegetables before adding them to your slow cooker. Putting frozen meat into a slow cooker could cause bad bacteria to grow in your pot, making it inedible. Some recipes call for browning your meat or sautéing veggies before adding them to the slow cooker; we recommend doing this right before you're ready to add ingredients. When placing ingredients into the slow cooker, put tougher meat and heartier root vegetables in first, on the bottom of the insert. More delicate and fast-cooking ingredients, like broccoli, should go on top.

It also helps to prep your ingredients the night before and refrigerate them overnight to save time the next day. However, don't store the ingredients in the slow cooker insert while being refrigerated. Remember, this could cause your insert to crack when heated up or take too long to rise in temperature! Of course, you could also prep your meal the day of. It's your kitchen!

It's necessary to be aware of the potential food dangers when cooking with a slow cooker. Never delay starting your slow cooker after ingredients have entered the pot. Start your slow cooker immediately. Always fully thaw meats before placing them into the slow cooker. You can do this by planning ahead and thawing your meat in the fridge, or by putting the meat in cold water (while still in its packaging). Thawing times vary depending on the method.

Always refrigerate your slow cooker meal within two hours after it's finished, or keep the slow cooker on a warm setting if continuing to serve food. But be cautious of the warm setting— you don't want to overcook your dish! Try to keep the warm setting on for a minimum of two hours and maximum of four hours. Make sure your meal

{ Be sure to properly thaw any frozen meat you use for recipes. Putting frozen meat in your slow cooker could cause bacteria to grow.

is fully cooled before putting it in the refrigerator. If you wish to freeze your dish, fill an airtight container to avoid freezer burn and ensure freshness when reheated. Consume within three months of freezing.

Always place meats on the bottom of the slow cooker to make sure they are closest to the heat source, and always keep your lid on unless otherwise specified by the recipe. This ensures even cooking. If you take off your lid, it releases heat. It's recommended that you push cooking time back 30 minutes if the lid is removed.

Always check your meat's temperature upon finishing (unless the meat is shredded). The recommended minimum temperature for most meats is 145°F. For specific meat temperatures, use the chart at right.

If you haven't used your slow cooker in a while or you have just bought a new one and want to make sure it works, you can do a simple test to avoid any mishaps. Fill your cooker halfway with cool water. Turn the slow cooker on low and "cook" the water for 8 hours. Remember, do not remove the lid while cooking! When time is up, remove the lid and check the water temperature using a thermometer. If the water has reached 185°F, you're good to go! If it doesn't, your slow cooker may not be heating correctly. If it goes over 185°F, your cooker may cook hotter than the average slow cooker.

Meat	Internal temperature
Poultry	165°F (75°C)
Poultry, ground	165°F (75°C)
Beef, ground	160°F (70°C)
Beef, steak or roast	145°F (65°C)
Veal	145°F (65°C)
Lamb, ground	160°F (70°C)
Lamb, chops	145°F (65°C)
Mutton	145°F (65°C)
Pork	145°F (65°C)
Ham	145°F (65°C)
Ham, precooked and reheated	165°F (75°C)
Venison, ground	160°F (70°C)
Venison, steak or roast	145°F (65°C)
Rabbit	160°F (70°C)
Bison, ground	160°F (70°C)
Bison, steak or roast	145°F (65°C)

Prepare your food and meats carefully before you start cooking so you can let the slow cooker do all the hard work without any risks.

Soups & Stews

Slow cookers are perhaps best known for producing delicious, rich soups, stews, and chowders. Perfect for a cozy day in, or even for taking to a party, the soups in this section will impress any guest.

HOMEMADE STOCK

These recipes are guidelines to get you started—you can use any vegetables, herbs, and seasonings that you like.

Vegetable Stock

vegetarian

INGREDIENTS

Chopped fresh vegetables (any combination), as needed

Salt, to taste

5 or 6 sprigs fresh thyme

1 small bunch fresh parsley

Black peppercorns

2 bay leaves

INSTRUCTIONS

1. Fill a big slow cooker about two-thirds full with the fresh vegetables, sprinkle with salt, and add enough water to cover.

2. Toss in the thyme, parsley, black peppercorns, and bay leaves. Cover and cook on high 5 hours.

3. Strain through cheesecloth or a fine-mesh strainer into a big bowl; discard solids and strain again.

4. Use the liquid in place of canned vegetable stock. Store in mason jars or freezer containers. Keeps well in the fridge for a few days or in the freezer for a few months.

Save and Recycle

You can use beautiful fresh vegetables in these recipes if you'd like, or save up vegetable scraps and trimmings in a big freezer bag in your freezer until you have enough for a batch of stock or broth.

Save bits and pieces of veggies–everything from the ends of onions (remove the papery skin first if you'd like) to the veggies in your crisper drawer that you keep ignoring because they're shriveled. When you're ready to cook, just dump the contents of the bag into your slow cooker and follow the guidelines on these pages. You can save up bones too, but keep chicken and beef ones separate.

Chicken Stock

INGREDIENTS

Leftover chicken bones (either raw or cooked without sauce)

1 onion

4 carrots

4 celery ribs

2 bay leaves

Black peppercorns, to taste

4 cloves garlic

1 teaspoon salt

TIP: To make chicken broth, use meaty chicken pieces instead of just the bones.

INSTRUCTIONS

1. Toss the leftover chicken bones into a big slow cooker.

2. Chop up the onion, carrots, and celery ribs and add to the cooker along with bay leaves, black peppercorns, garlic, and salt; add water to cover. Cover and cook on low for 8 hours.

3. Strain through a colander into a big bowl; discard solids and strain again through cheesecloth or a fine-mesh strainer into a bowl, discarding solids; cover and refrigerate liquid overnight.

4. The next day, skim off congealed fat. Store the liquid in mason jars or freezer containers. Keeps well in the fridge for a few days or in the freezer for a few months. Use in place of canned chicken stock.

Beef Stock

INGREDIENTS

Beef bones (browned first if raw, or cooked without sauce)

1 onion

4 carrots

4 celery ribs

2 bay leaves

Black peppercorns, to taste

4 cloves garlic

1 teaspoon salt

2 tablespoons apple cider vinegar

INSTRUCTIONS

1. Put the beef bones into a slow cooker with the same assortment of vegetables, herbs, and seasonings used in Chicken Stock (recipe on page 16), adding the apple cider vinegar with the water.

2. Cook, strain, skim, and store as indicated for Chicken Stock. Use in place of canned beef stock.

3. To make beef broth, use meaty beef pieces instead of just the bones.

Crab Chowder with Roasted Veggies

> *Makes about 7 cups*

INGREDIENTS

1 tablespoon canola oil

1½ cups frozen corn

1 onion, chopped

1 celery rib, chopped

1 (10 ounce) jar roasted red peppers, drained and chopped

1 clove garlic, minced

¼ teaspoon cayenne pepper

¼ teaspoon ground thyme

2 teaspoons Old Bay seasoning

2 (14.5 ounce) cans chicken broth

¼ cup flour

¾ cup heavy cream

4 ounces fontina cheese, cubed

1 (6 ounce) package refrigerated lump crabmeat, flaked

INSTRUCTIONS

1. Heat the oil in a big skillet; add the corn, onion, and celery and sauté until lightly browned.

2. Dump everything from the skillet into a 3-quart slow cooker. Add the roasted peppers, garlic, cayenne pepper, thyme, Old Bay, and broth. Cover and cook on low 6 hours (high, 3 hours).

3. Combine the flour and cream in a small, lidded container; put on the lid, shake it, then stir slowly into the soup.

4. Cook 30 minutes longer.

5. Stir in the cheese and crab and let stand until the cheese is melted. Give it a stir and serve it up. Enjoy!

Slow & Easy French Onion Soup

> *Makes about 11 cups*

INGREDIENTS

¼ cup unsalted butter, sliced

6 sprigs fresh thyme

1 bay leaf

16 cups (about 5 pounds) sweet
  onions, sliced

1 tablespoon sugar

6 cups beef stock

2 tablespoons red wine vinegar

1½ teaspoons salt

1 teaspoon black pepper

11 French bread slices

Irish cheddar cheese, shredded,
  as needed

INSTRUCTIONS

1. Coat a 6-quart slow cooker with cooking spray and toss in butter, fresh thyme, bay leaf, and onions; sprinkle with sugar. Cover and cook on high 8 hours.

2. Remove and discard the herbs. Stir in beef stock, red wine vinegar, salt, and black pepper. Cover and cook on high 30 minutes.

3. Preheat the broiler.

4. Spritz cooking spray on both sides of French bread slices (one slice for each serving of soup) and broil until toasted on both sides.

5. Ladle soup into heatproof bowls set on a rimmed baking sheet; top each with toasted bread and the shredded Irish cheddar cheese. Broil until the cheese melts. Serve and enjoy!

Savory Beef Stew

> *Makes about 12 cups*

INGREDIENTS

2 (1 ounce) packages dry onion soup mix

½ teaspoon paprika

2 pounds beef stew meat, trimmed and cut into bite-size pieces

5 potatoes, peeled and diced

3 cups baby carrots, halved

1 onion, chopped

2 (10 ounce) cans cream of celery soup

1 cup ketchup

Black pepper, to taste

INSTRUCTIONS

1. In a big, zippered plastic bag, mix the onion soup mix and paprika.

2. Add the beef stew meat and shake to coat.

3. Toss the coated meat into a 5-quart slow cooker.

4. Add the potatoes, baby carrots, and onion.

5. Stir together the cream of celery soup and ketchup and pour into the cooker; season with the black pepper.

6. Stir it up, cover, and cook on low for 8 hours (high, 4 hours), until everything is tender.

Creamy Broccoli-Cheese Soup

> *Makes about 8 cups*

INGREDIENTS

¼ cup butter

¼ cup flour

3 cups whole milk

3 cups chicken broth

1 small yellow onion, chopped

3 cloves garlic, smashed

4 cups fresh broccoli florets

2 ounces cream cheese, cubed

1 teaspoon each salt and
    black pepper

½ teaspoon Italian seasoning

3 cups shredded cheddar cheese,
    plus more for serving

INSTRUCTIONS

1. Melt the butter in a saucepan over medium heat and whisk in the flour until thick and smooth. Whisk in the milk until fully incorporated.

2. Cook until slightly thickened, whisking often, then remove from the heat.

3. Pour the broth into a 4-quart slow cooker. Stir in the onion, garlic, broccoli, cream cheese, salt, black pepper, Italian seasoning, and thickened milk. Cover and cook on low 6 hours (high, 3 hours).

4. Turn off the cooker and stir in 3 cups of cheese; let set until the cheese melts. Top each serving with more cheese.

Delicious Duo: Pair this with Creamy Broccoli-Cheddar Soup!

Cheesy Grilled Steak Sandwiches

> *Serves* 4

INGREDIENTS

½ pound boneless ribeye steak

½ cup steak sauce

¼ cup BBQ sauce

1½ teaspoons minced garlic

Salt and black pepper, to taste

1 tomato, sliced

Olive oil, as needed

8 slices potato bread

Shredded mozzarella cheese, as needed

Crumbled Feta cheese, as needed

Fresh chives, as needed

Parsley, as needed

INSTRUCTIONS

1. Marinate the ribeye steak for a couple of hours in a mixture of the steak sauce, BBQ sauce, and minced garlic.

2. Discard the marinade, season the steak with salt, and grill until done to your liking; tent with foil, set aside for 5 minutes, then thinly slice.

3. Drizzle the tomato slices with olive oil, and season with the salt and black pepper; grill until lightly browned on both sides.

4. Grill four slices of the potato bread on one side; flip and add some shredded mozzarella and crumbled feta to two slices.

5. When the cheese is melty, remove from the grill. To the cheese, add the chopped fresh chives and parsley, grilled tomatoes, and steak slices; top with the remaining toasted bread.

6. Cut in half and share.

Beefy Chipotle Chili

> *Makes about 9 cups*

INGREDIENTS

2 tablespoons butter

1 pound lean ground beef

¾ cup each diced onion, celery, and green bell pepper

2 cloves garlic, minced

1 (8 ounce) can tomato sauce

2 tomatoes, chopped

2 (15 ounce) cans kidney beans, drained and rinsed

1 (15 ounce) can cannellini beans, drained and rinsed

1½ teaspoons chili powder

½ to 1 teaspoon chipotle chili powder

1 teaspoon salt

¾ teaspoon each dried basil, oregano, and parsley

¼ teaspoon black pepper

A few dashes hot sauce

1 (5.5 ounce) can V8 juice

1½ cups beef stock

Crumbled cotija or queso fresco cheese, for topping

Sliced green onions, for topping

INSTRUCTIONS

1. Melt the butter in a big skillet and add the beef, onion, celery, bell pepper, and garlic.

2. Cook until the meat is no longer pink, crumbling it as it cooks; drain.

3. Dump everything from the skillet into a 3-quart slow cooker. Stir in the tomato sauce, tomatoes, all the beans, both kinds of chili powder, salt, basil, oregano, parsley, black pepper, hot sauce, V8, and stock. Cover and cook on low for 8 hours (high, 4 hours).

4. Top each serving with the cheese and green onions. Enjoy!

Canadian Bacon Chowder

> *Makes about 8 cups*

INGREDIENTS

2 cups Yukon gold potatoes, diced

1 carrot, diced

1 cup leeks, chopped

½ teaspoon minced garlic

4 cups chicken broth

½ cup uncooked medium
    pearled barley

1 bay leaf

¼ teaspoon dried thyme, crushed

Black pepper, to taste

6 ounces Canadian bacon, diced

4 ounces fresh mushrooms, diced

1 (5 ounce) can evaporated milk

¼ cup half-and-half

INSTRUCTIONS

1. In a 3-quart slow cooker, combine the potatoes, carrot, leeks (white and light green parts), garlic, chicken broth, barley, bay leaf, thyme, black pepper, Canadian bacon, and mushrooms; stir to blend.

2. Cover and cook on low 6 hours (high, 3 hours).

3. Stir in the evaporated milk and half-and-half. Leave the lid off and cook 15 minutes longer or until heated through.

4. Serve and enjoy!

Cabbage Roll Soup

> *Makes about 14 cups*

INGREDIENTS

2 tablespoons olive oil

½ cup onion, chopped

½ cup shallot, chopped

2 pounds lean ground beef

1 teaspoon minced garlic

1 teaspoon salt

1 teaspoon black pepper

1 teaspoon dried parsley

½ teaspoon each cayenne pepper
   and dried oregano

½ head cauliflower, coarsely chopped

1 cabbage, coarsely chopped

1 (16 ounce) jar marinara sauce

5 cups beef broth

Shredded Parmesan cheese,
   for topping

INSTRUCTIONS

1. Heat olive oil in a skillet over medium-high heat.

2. Add onion and shallots and cook until softened.

3. Add ground beef and garlic and cook until the meat is browned, crumbling it as it cooks; drain.

4. Dump everything from the skillet into a 7-quart slow cooker. Sprinkle in salt, black pepper, parsley, cayenne pepper, and oregano.

5. Add cauliflower, cabbage, marinara sauce, and beef broth. Stir until well mixed

6. Cover and cook on low 6 hours (high, 3 hours) or until cabbage is tender.

7. Sprinkle each serving with shredded Parmesan cheese and serve.

Mexican Rice & Bean Soup

> *Makes about 7 cups*

vegetarian

INGREDIENTS

1 tablespoon olive oil

1 small onion, diced

2 cloves minced garlic

½ teaspoon each ground cumin and chili powder

1 (15.25 ounce) can black beans, drained and rinsed

1 (14.5 ounce) can petite diced tomatoes with green chiles (don't drain)

1 (10 ounce) can petite diced tomatoes with lime and cilantro (don't drain)

1 (11 ounce) can white corn (don't drain)

½ cup uncooked long-grain white rice

3 cups water

¼ teaspoon each salt and black pepper

¼ cup fresh cilantro, chopped

Juice of 1 lime

Guacamole, for topping

Shredded pepper jack cheese, for topping

INSTRUCTIONS

1. In a small skillet, heat the oil over medium-high heat. Then, sauté the onion, garlic, cumin, and chili powder in hot oil about 5 minutes.

2. Pour everything from the skillet into a 3-quart slow cooker.

3. Toss in the beans, all the tomatoes, corn, and rice. Add the water and season with salt and black pepper. Stir everything together.

4. Cook on low for 6 hours (high, 3 hours) or until the rice is tender.

5. Turn off the cooker and stir in the cilantro and lime juice.

6. Top each serving with the guacamole and cheese and enjoy.

Crockin' Taco Soup

> *Makes about 9 cups*

INGREDIENTS

1 pound ground pork

1 (16 ounce) jar salsa

1 (4 ounce) can diced green chiles

1 (15 ounce) can black beans, drained and rinsed

1 cup frozen white corn

1 onion, diced

½ bell pepper, diced

1 (1 ounce) package taco seasoning mix

1 teaspoon ground cumin

4 cups chicken broth, divided

3 tablespoons flour

Sour cream, for topping

Shredded cheddar cheese, for topping

INSTRUCTIONS

1. Cook the ground pork in medium-high heat until done, crumbling it as it cooks; drain and put into a 3-quart slow cooker.

2. Add the salsa, diced green chiles, black beans, frozen white corn, onion, bell pepper, taco seasoning mix, cumin, and 3 cups of the chicken broth.

3. Whisk together the flour and 1 cup of the chicken broth until smooth; slowly stir into the cooker. Cook on low 6 hours (high, 3 hours).

4. Top each serving with the sour cream, shredded cheddar cheese, and any of your other favorite taco toppings.

Vegetable Beef & Barley

> *Makes about 15 cups*

INGREDIENTS

1 teaspoon each seasoned salt, onion powder, and garlic powder

1½ pounds beef stew meat, trimmed and cut into bite-size pieces

2 tablespoons canola oil

4 cups water

3 Yukon gold potatoes, diced

1 cup each carrots and celery, sliced

½ cup onion, chopped

1 tablespoon French onion-flavored beef bouillon granules (such as Wyler's Shakers)

1 (15.25 ounce) can whole kernel corn, drained

1 (14.5 ounce) can diced tomatoes (don't drain)

1 cup tomato juice

¾ cup uncooked medium pearled barley

1½ teaspoons salt

1 teaspoon black pepper

1 cup frozen peas, thawed

INSTRUCTIONS

1. In a big, zippered plastic bag, combine the seasoned salt, onion powder, and garlic powder. Shake it up to blend.

2. Toss in the beef pieces and shake until thoroughly coated.

3. Heat the oil in a big skillet. Add the coated meat and cook until browned on all sides; drain.

4. Toss the cooked meat into a 5-quart slow cooker and add the water, potatoes, carrots, celery, onion, and bouillon. Cover and cook on low 6 hours (high, 3 hours).

5. Stir in the corn, tomatoes, tomato juice, barley, salt, and black pepper. Cover and cook on low 2 hours longer or until the barley is tender.

6. Stir in the peas and serve.

Corn Chowder with a Kick

❯ *Makes about 13 cups*

INGREDIENTS

2 (14.75 ounce) cans cream-style corn

2 cups frozen sweet corn

2 (10.5 ounce) cans cream of mushroom soup

2 (4 ounce) cans chopped green chiles

2 cups frozen O'Brien hash browns

2 cups cooked ham, cubed

1 cup frozen onions, chopped

2 tablespoons butter, sliced

2 tablespoons hot sauce

2 teaspoons dried parsley

1 teaspoon chili powder

3 cups milk

Salt and black pepper, to taste

Crisply cooked bacon, crumbled, for topping

INSTRUCTIONS

1. In a 4-quart slow cooker, stir together the cream-style corn, frozen sweet corn, cream of mushroom soup, chopped green chiles, frozen O'Brien hash browns, ham, frozen onions, butter, hot sauce, dried parsley, chili powder, and milk.

2. Season with the salt and black pepper.

3. Cover and cook on low 6 hours (high, 3 hours).

4. Top each serving with a handful of the bacon. Serve and enjoy!

Tomato-Basil Soup

> *Makes about 12 cups*

vegetarian

INGREDIENTS

3 (15 ounce) cans petite diced tomatoes (don't drain)

1 cup each celery, onion, and carrots, finely chopped

3 cups vegetable broth

½ cup butter

½ cup flour

2 cups half-and-half

½ cup shredded Parmesan cheese, plus more for topping

½ cup shredded Asiago cheese, plus more for topping

1 teaspoon salt

½ teaspoon ground oregano

¼ cup fresh basil, chopped

Black pepper, to taste

INSTRUCTIONS

1. In a 4-quart slow cooker, combine the tomatoes, celery, onion, carrots, and vegetable broth. Cover and cook on low 6 hours (high, 3 hours).

2. Melt the butter in a big saucepan over medium heat and then whisk in the flour until thick and smooth. Slowly whisk in the half-and-half plus 1 to 2 cups of the soup from the cooker; whisk until well blended.

3. Pour the blended mixture into the cooker, add both cheeses, and stir until melted.

4. Stir in the salt, oregano, basil, and black pepper; cover and cook on low 30 minutes longer.

5. Blend the soup with an immersion blender until nice and smooth.

6. Toss a little extra cheese onto each serving and enjoy.

Delicious Duo:

Pair this with Tomato-Basil Soup!

Pesto Chicken on Ciabatta

> *Serves* 4

INGREDIENTS

¾ pound chicken breast

Montreal chicken seasoning, to taste

4 ciabatta rolls

2 tablespoons mayonnaise

2 tablespoons sun-dried tomato pesto

Shredded mozzarella cheese

Red peppers, roasted and sliced, for topping

Guacamole, for topping

Fresh basil leaves, for topping

INSTRUCTIONS

1. Season the chicken breast with the Montreal chicken seasoning and broil until done; thinly slice.

2. Cut the ciabatta rolls in half; broil until toasted.

3. Mix the mayonnaise and sun-dried tomato pesto and spread on cut side of buns. Arrange the chicken on bun bottoms, add the shredded mozzarella, and broil until cheese melts.

4. Top with roasted red peppers, a slather of guacamole, and fresh basil leaves. Add toasted bun tops. Serve warm and enjoy.

Old-Fashioned Beef & Noodle Soup

> *Makes about 8 cups*

INGREDIENTS

2 teaspoons olive oil

1 pound beef stew meat, cut into bite-size pieces

1 cup onion, chopped

1 cup each fresh mushrooms and carrots, sliced

1 red bell pepper, diced

1 (1 ounce) package dry beefy onion soup mix

2 tablespoons tomato paste

1 tablespoon Worcestershire sauce

1 teaspoon minced garlic

Salt and black pepper, to taste

6 cups water

2½ cups uncooked extra-wide homemade-style egg noodles

INSTRUCTIONS

1. Heat oil over medium heat in a skillet and add the stew meat and onion, cooking until the meat is browned on all sides; drain.

2. Toss the meat and onion into a 3-quart slow cooker. Add the mushrooms, carrots, bell pepper, dry soup mix, tomato paste, Worcestershire sauce, garlic, salt, and black pepper.

3. Pour in water and give it a quick stir. Cover and cook on low for 6 to 7 hours (high, 3 to 3½ hours), until the vegetables are tender.

4. Stir in the noodles, cover, and cook 20 to 30 minutes longer or until the noodles are soft. Ladle into bowls and enjoy!

Bean, Andouille & Spinach Soup

> *Makes about 10 cups*

INGREDIENTS

1 (13.5 ounce) package andouille sausage, sliced

2 (15 ounce) cans northern white beans, drained and rinsed

4 cups chicken broth

2 cups salsa

1 cup frozen carrots

½ cup red onion, diced

½ cup celery, sliced

½ cup parsley, chopped

2 teaspoons Creole seasoning

2 teaspoons garlic powder

2 teaspoons onion powder

2 teaspoons black pepper

3 cups baby spinach

INSTRUCTIONS

1. Brown the andouille sausage in a skillet; drain and dump into a 4-quart slow cooker.

2. Add the northern white beans, chicken broth, salsa, frozen carrots, red onion, celery, parsley, Creole seasoning, garlic powder, onion powder, and black pepper.

3. Cover and cook on low 8 hours (high, 4 hours).

4. Stir in the baby spinach and cook 15 minutes longer or until the spinach is just wilted. Serve and enjoy!

Turkey & Wild Rice Soup

> *Makes about 14 cups*

INGREDIENTS

1 pound cooked turkey, diced

1 cup uncooked wild rice

1 cup mushrooms, sliced

1 (10 ounce) package frozen mixed vegetables (carrots, onions, celery, and peppers)

6 cups chicken stock, divided

4 cups water

2 tablespoons chicken bouillon powder

2 tablespoons dry chicken soup base

Salt, to taste, plus ½ teaspoon

Black pepper, to taste, plus ½ teaspoon

¼ cup butter

½ cup flour

1 cup each heavy cream and half-and- half

1 tablespoon dried parsley

1 cup frozen mixed vegetables (corn, peas, and green beans)

INSTRUCTIONS

1. In a 5-quart slow cooker, mix the turkey, wild rice, mushrooms, frozen mixed vegetables, 4 cups of the chicken stock, water, chicken bouillon powder, dry chicken soup base, and the salt and black pepper.

2. Cover and cook on low 6 hours (high, 3 hours).

3. Melt the butter in a saucepan over medium heat; whisk in flour until smooth.

4. Stir in the heavy cream and half-and-half, 2 cups of the chicken stock, parsley, and ½ teaspoon each of the salt and black pepper and cook until thickened, whisking constantly; add to the cooker along with the frozen mixed vegetables.

5. Cook uncovered on low for 30 minutes, until thickened. Serve and enjoy!

Cheesy Potato Soup

> *Makes about 10 cups*

INGREDIENTS

1 (32 ounce) packaged frozen diced hash browns

½ cup frozen chopped onion

1 celery rib, chopped

4 cups chicken broth

1 cups water

3 tablespoons flour

1 cup milk

½ teaspoon black pepper

1 cup each American and cheddar cheeses, cubed

Shredded cheddar cheese, for topping

Bacon, cooked and crumbled, for topping

Chives, chopped, for topping

INSTRUCTIONS

1. Put the hash browns, onion, celery, broth, and water into a 3-quart slow cooker. Cover and cook on low 8 hours (high, 4 hours).

2. Whisk together the flour, milk, and black pepper until smooth; stir into the soup. Cover and cook on high 30 minutes longer, until the soup thickens.

3. Stir in both the cubed cheeses, cover, and let stand until melted.

4. Top each serving with the shredded cheese, bacon, and chives. Serve and enjoy.

Delicious Duo:

Pair this with Cheesy Potato Soup!

Buffalo Chicken Roll-Ups

> *Makes about 12*

INGREDIENTS

1 large chicken breast half, cooked and shredded

½ (8 ounce) package cream cheese, softened

⅓ cup buffalo wing sauce, plus more for serving

2 tablespoons blue cheese dressing, plus more for serving

3 green onions, thinly sliced

1 (8 ounce) tube refrigerated crescent dough

INSTRUCTIONS

1. Preheat the oven to 375°F.

2. Mix the chicken with the cream cheese, buffalo wing sauce, blue cheese dressing, and green onions.

3. Unroll the refrigerated crescent dough sheet on parchment paper and spread evenly with the chicken mixture.

4. Starting with one long side, roll up and pinch the edges to seal in the filling. Use unflavored dental floss to cut the roll into 1-inch slices; set the slices on an ungreased cookie sheet. Bake 15 to 18 minutes or until nicely browned.

5. Serve with the leftover wing sauce or blue cheese dressing for dipping if you'd like.

Beef Fajita Soup

> *Makes about 8 cups*

INGREDIENTS

1½ pounds boneless beef sirloin steak, trimmed

1 teaspoon each ground cumin, paprika, and black pepper

1 teaspoon sea salt

½ to 1 tablespoon chili powder

1 teaspoon olive oil

1 each yellow, orange, and green bell pepper, chopped

½ jalapeño pepper, sliced, plus more for serving (optional)

1 cup fresh salsa

2 teaspoons minced garlic

Juice of 1 lime

4 cups beef broth

Diced avocado, for serving

INSTRUCTIONS

1. Put the steak in the freezer for 30 minutes to make it easier to slice, then cut it into thin, bite-size pieces.

2. Mix the cumin, paprika, black pepper, sea salt, and chili powder in a zippered plastic bag; toss in the meat and shake to coat.

3. In a skillet, heat the oil and then cook the meat until browned and then toss into a 3-quart slow cooker.

4. Add the bell peppers, jalapeño (if using), salsa, garlic, lime juice, and broth; stir. Cover and cook on low 6 hours (high, 3 hours), until everything is tender.

5. Top each serving with the avocado and more jalapeño slices.

To make tortilla chips, cut 8 corn tortillas into 6 wedges each. Heat 2 cups canola oil to 365°F in a big skillet. Fry the wedges a few at a time in the hot oil until crisp; transfer to paper towels and immediately brush with lime juice and sprinkle with a little sea salt and chili powder. Serve the chips with the soup.

Hearty Ham & Bean Soup

> *Makes about 9 cups*

INGREDIENTS

1 large yellow onion, chopped

2 celery ribs, chopped

1 meaty ham bone or several ham hocks

1 (1 pound) package dry 15-bean mix, picked over and rinsed

2 bay leaves

1 tablespoon minced garlic

Black pepper, to taste

Vegetable broth, as needed (6 to 8 cups)

INSTRUCTIONS

1. Put the onion and celery ribs into a 3-quart slow cooker.

2. Add the meaty ham bone or several ham hocks, 15-bean mix, bay leaves, and minced garlic; season with black pepper.

3. Pour in enough vegetable broth to cover the vegetables. Cover and cook on low for 8 hours, until everything is tender.

4. Remove and discard the bay leaves; remove the meat, discarding the fat and bones. Shred or chop the meat and return to the cooker, stirring to combine. Serve and enjoy.

Easy Minestrone

> *Makes about 12 cups*

INGREDIENTS

1 pound ground pork sausage

1 teaspoon garlic powder

2 (19 ounce) cans ready-to-eat minestrone soup

2 (15 ounce) cans ranch-style beans

1 (15.25 ounce) can whole kernel corn, drained

1 (28 ounce) can crushed tomatoes with basil

Sour cream, for topping

Shredded cheese, (any kind) for topping

INSTRUCTIONS

1. In a skillet, cook the ground pork sausage, crumbling it as it cooks; drain.

2. Put the meat into a 4-quart slow cooker. Stir in the garlic powder, minestrone soup, beans, corn, and crushed tomatoes with basil.

3. Cover and cook on low 5 hours (high, 2½ hours).

4. Top each serving with the sour cream and your favorite shredded cheese.

Creamy Cauliflower-Parsnip Soup

> *Makes about 7 cups*

INGREDIENTS

1 head cauliflower, cut into florets

3 large parsnips, peeled and sliced

2 teaspoons minced garlic

1 tablespoon chicken bouillon powder

3 cups water

2 teaspoons coconut oil

1 large onion, thinly sliced

Salt and black pepper, to taste

1 Granny Smith apple

½ cup coconut milk or heavy cream

INSTRUCTIONS

1. In a 3-quart slow cooker, layer the cauliflower, parsnips, and garlic. Mix the bouillon powder with water and pour into the cooker, adding more water if needed so veggies are just covered. Cover and cook on low for 7 hours (high, 3½ hours).

2. About 30 minutes before the end of cooking time, heat the oil over medium heat in a big skillet. Add the onion and a pinch of salt and cook until just beginning to brown.

3. Dice the apple and toss it into the skillet with the onion; cook for 30 minutes or until the onion is golden brown, stirring occasionally.

4. At the end of cooking time, stir the coconut milk or heavy cream into the cooker and season with the salt and black pepper.

5. Puree with an immersion blender until the desired consistency is reached.

6. Ladle into bowls and top each with some of the onion mixture.

Pair this with Creamy Cauliflower-Parsnip Soup!

Loaded Italian Grilled Cheese

> *Serves 8*

INGREDIENTS

1 (13 ounce) package cooked Italian herb sausage, sliced

1 each red and orange bell pepper, sliced

1 small yellow onion, sliced

2 tablespoons butter

1 tablespoon olive oil

8 slices ciabatta bread

Dried parsley, for serving

Shredded enchilado, Gouda, and Munster cheeses, for serving

INSTRUCTIONS

1. Sauté the Italian herb sausage along with the bell peppers and onion in hot oil on medium-high heat until vegetables have softened.

2. Melt the butter in a separate skillet on medium-low heat and add four slices of the ciabatta bread; top with the parsley and shredded cheeses.

3. Add some of the sausage mixture, even more cheese, and another bread slice to each. Brown both sides. Cut in half and share.

Turkey Pot Pie in a Bowl

> *Makes about 10 cups*

INGREDIENTS

1 tablespoon olive oil

2 pounds turkey meat, cut into bite-size pieces

1½ teaspoons salt

1½ teaspoons black pepper

1 small yellow onion, diced

1 teaspoon minced garlic

3 celery ribs, diced

1 (16 ounce) bag frozen peas and carrots

1½ cup Yukon gold potatoes, diced

3 sprigs fresh thyme

6 cups chicken stock

¾ cups half-and-half

¼ cup flour

Biscuits, for serving

INSTRUCTIONS

1. Heat the oil in a big skillet and add the meat. Cook until golden brown; drain.

2. Toss the meat into a 3-quart slow cooker and season with the salt and black pepper. Add the onion, garlic, celery, peas and carrots, potatoes, thyme, and stock.

3. In a small, lidded container, combine the half-and-half and flour; put on the lid, shake well, and stir slowly into soup.

4. Cover and cook on low 6 hours (high, 3 hours) or until the potatoes are tender. Serve with biscuits and enjoy.

Chicken Tortilla Soup

> *Makes about 8 cups*

INGREDIENTS

1 (11 ounce) can condensed fiesta nacho cheese soup

1 (10.7 ounce) can cream of chicken soup

2 (10 ounce) cans chunk chicken, drained

1¼ cups enchilada sauce

1 (4.25 ounce) can chopped green chiles

2⅔ cups milk

Shredded cheddar cheese, for topping

Sour cream, for topping

Tortilla strips, for topping

Green onion, sliced, for topping

INSTRUCTIONS

1. In a 3-quart slow cooker, stir together the fiesta nacho cheese soup, cream of chicken soup, chunk chicken, enchilada sauce, and chopped green chiles.

2. Cook on low 3 hours.

3. Stir in the milk and cook 30 minutes longer, until hot.

4. Top each serving with the shredded cheddar cheese, sour cream, tortilla strips, and sliced green onions.

Almost Lasagna Soup

> *Makes about 10 cups*

INGREDIENTS

1 (28 ounce) can diced tomatoes

1 (6 ounce) can tomato paste

3 cups vegetable stock

1 (12 ounce) package frozen veggie
   crumbles (like Morning Star
   Farms Grillers)

1 tablespoon minced garlic

1 tablespoon dried parsley

1 tablespoon dried basil

½ cup onion, chopped

2 (5.5 ounce) cans V8 juice

1 teaspoon salt

1 teaspoon black pepper

1 cup water

2 cups uncooked Mafalda pasta

Shredded mozzarella cheese, for topping

Shredded Parmesan cheese, for topping

INSTRUCTIONS

1. In a 3-quart slow cooker, mix the diced tomatoes and tomato paste.

2. Stir in the vegetable stock, frozen veggie crumbles, garlic, parsley, basil, onion, V8 juice, and salt and black pepper.

3. Cover and cook on low 8 hours (high, 4 hours).

4. Add water and the uncooked Mafalda pasta (mini lasagna noodles); stir to combine.

5. Cover and cook 30 minutes longer, until pasta is tender.

6. Top each serving with the shredded cheeses.

Granny Smith Squash Soup

> *Makes about 8 cups*

INGREDIENTS

1 tablespoon olive oil

1 large onion, cut into chunks

8 cups (about 2 medium) butternut squash, peeled, seeded, and cubed

2 tablespoons brown sugar

¾ teaspoon salt

¾ teaspoon cinnamon

⅛ teaspoon white pepper

3 cups chicken broth

2 large Granny Smith apples, divided

¾ cup milk

1 (6 ounce) container plain Greek yogurt, plus more for serving

Bacon, cooked and crumbled, for topping

INSTRUCTIONS

1. In a skillet, heat the oil and then cook onion until softened. Transfer to a 6-quart slow cooker and add the squash, brown sugar, salt, cinnamon, white pepper, and broth; peel and chop one of the apples and add it to the cooker.

2. Stir, cover, and cook on low 6 hours (high, 3 hours), until squash is tender.

3. Use an immersion blender to blend the soup until silky smooth. Stir in the milk and 6 ounces of yogurt.

4. Cut the remaining apple into matchsticks.

5. Top each serving of soup with more yogurt, some bacon, and the apple matchsticks.

Delicious Duo: **Pair this with Granny Smith Squash Soup!**

Turkey-Brie Sandwiches

> *Serves* 4

INGREDIENTS

¼ cup mayonnaise

¼ cup sriracha mayonnaise

½ teaspoon chili powder

8 slices ciabatta bread

Oven-roasted deli turkey, sliced, as needed

Fresh peaches, sliced, as needed

Brie cheese, sliced, as needed

Arugula, as needed

INSTRUCTIONS

1. Preheat the oven to 375°F.

2. Stir together the mayonnaise, sriracha mayonnaise, and chili powder; set aside.

3. Set four slices of the ciabatta bread on a baking sheet; on two of the bread slices, layer turkey slices, peach slices, and some Brie cheese (the other two bread slices will toast without toppings).

4. Bake 10 to 15 minutes, until the cheese melts. Put some arugula on the melty cheese, spread the set-aside mayo mixture over the plain toasted bread, and put sandwiches together.

5. Cut in half and share.

For a sweet version of this sandwich, omit the mayo mixture and arugula, and sprinkle brown sugar over the cheese before baking.

Southwest Chicken Stew

> *Makes about 10 cups*

INGREDIENTS

2 baking potatoes (3 to 4 cups), peeled and cut into chunks

1 (12 ounce) package frozen Southwest vegetable blend

2 each celery ribs and carrots, sliced

1 onion, sliced

1 teaspoon minced garlic

1 cup spicy salsa

1½ teaspoons ground cumin

1 teaspoon chili powder

½ teaspoon black pepper

Hot sauce, to taste

2 boneless, skinless chicken breasts

2 boneless, skinless chicken thighs

3½ cups chicken broth

1 teaspoon salt

INSTRUCTIONS

1. In a 4-quart slow cooker, stir together the potatoes, vegetable blend, celery, carrots, onion, garlic, salsa, cumin, chili powder, black pepper, and hot sauce.

2. Lay all the chicken pieces on top and pour in the broth. Cover and cook on high 4 hours.

3. Remove and shred the meat, sprinkle generously with salt, and return to the cooker.

4. Stir and serve.

TIP: Adjust the seasonings in this recipe to fit your taste. By adding frozen Southwest vegetables, you get instant added flavor. Zip and zing included.

Shortcut Meatball Stew

> *Makes about 12 cups*

INGREDIENTS

1 (14 ounce) bag cooked frozen homestyle meatballs

1 (15 ounce) can crushed tomatoes (don't drain)

1 (8 ounce) can tomato sauce

2 (14.5 ounce) cans beef broth

2 cups water

½ cup each frozen carrots, frozen pearl onions, frozen corn, shelled edamame, and bell pepper

1½ cups small shell pasta

Salt, to taste

Black pepper, to taste,

Garlic powder, to taste

Cayenne pepper, to taste

½ cup chopped fresh parsley

Crunchy bread, for serving

INSTRUCTIONS

1. Toss the cooked frozen homestyle meatballs into a 4-quart slow cooker.

2. Add the crushed tomatoes, tomato sauce, beef broth, water, frozen carrots, frozen pearl onions, frozen corn, shelled edamame, and bell pepper.

3. Cover and cook on low for 5 hours (high, 2½ hours) or until the vegetables are tender.

4. Stir the pasta into the cooker and season with salt, black pepper, garlic powder, and cayenne pepper.

5. Stir in the parsley and cook 45 minutes longer, until the pasta is cooked to perfection.

6. Serve with crunchy bread.

Buffalo Chicken Noodle Soup

> *Makes about 9 cups*

INGREDIENTS

2 cups shredded rotisserie chicken

4 each celery ribs and
   carrots, chopped

1 small yellow onion, chopped

2 teaspoons minced garlic

1½ tablespoons dry ranch
   dressing mix

½ cup buffalo wing sauce

6 cups chicken stock

2 tablespoons cornstarch

2 tablespoons cold water

Salt and black pepper, to taste

2½ cups uncooked wide egg noodles

¼ cup chopped fresh parsley

Blue cheese crumbles, for topping

INSTRUCTIONS

1. In a 3-quart slow cooker, mix the shredded rotisserie chicken, celery ribs, carrots, onion, garlic, ranch dressing mix, buffalo wing sauce, and chicken stock.

2. Cover and cook on low 6 hours (high, 3 hours), until the veggies are tender.

3. Whisk together the cornstarch and cold water until smooth, and stir into the cooker.

4. Season soup with salt and black pepper and add more wing sauce if you like it spicier.

5. Add the uncooked wide egg noodles and parsley. Cook for 10 minutes or until the noodles have softened.

6. Top each serving with blue cheese crumbles. Enjoy!

Chunky Couscous Soup

> *Makes about 10 cups*

vegetarian

INGREDIENTS

1 tablespoon butter

1 onion, finely chopped

1 green bell pepper, finely chopped

1 cup carrots, finely chopped

2 (15 ounce) cans kidney beans, drained and rinsed

1 cup uncooked couscous

1 (14.5 ounce) can stewed tomatoes (don't drain)

1 cup marinara sauce

1 teaspoon each salt and dried basil

¼ teaspoon black pepper

½ teaspoon cayenne pepper

4 cups vegetable stock

INSTRUCTIONS

1. Melt the butter in a big skillet. Add the onion, bell pepper, and carrots. Cook about 10 minutes.

2. Transfer everything from the skillet to a 3-quart slow cooker. Stir in the kidney beans, couscous, tomatoes, marinara sauce, salt, basil, black pepper, cayenne pepper, and stock.

3. Cover and cook on low 3 hours, until the vegetables are tender.

4. Turn off the cooker. Stir, cover, and let stand 30 minutes before serving to give the soup a chance to thicken up a bit.

5. Serve and enjoy!

Couscous [KOOS-koos]:

These little pearls of versatility can be eaten hot or cold, stirred into a salad or tucked into a sandwich, quick-cooked or tossed into a slow cooker to leisurely morph into the yummiest of comfort food. Enjoy!

Delicious Duo:

Pair this with Chunky Couscous Soup!

Veggie & Hummus Pita

> *Serves 4*

vegetarian

INGREDIENTS

1⅓ cups cherry tomatoes, halved

1 cucumber, chopped

1 small red onion, diced

Olive oil, as needed

Salt and black pepper, to taste

Hummus, as needed

4 flatbreads

Crumbled feta cheese, for topping

Black or green olives, sliced, for topping (optional)

INSTRUCTIONS

1. Toss the cherry tomatoes into a bowl with the cucumber and a small red onion; drizzle with a little olive oil and sprinkle with salt and black pepper to taste. Stir to blend.

2. Spread each of the four flatbreads with a good amount of your favorite hummus.

3. Divide the vegetable mixture evenly among the flatbreads and toss on a handful of feta cheese crumbles. Add the sliced black or green olives if you'd like.

4. Fold and eat.

Spicy Italian Sausage Soup

> *Makes about 11 cups*

INGREDIENTS

1 pound ground spicy Italian sausage

½ pound hickory-smoked bacon, chopped

4 cups water

4 cups chicken broth

1 large sweet potato, peeled and cubed

2 cloves garlic, crushed

1 small onion, chopped

2 cups fresh kale, chopped

1 cup heavy cream

Salt and black pepper, to taste

Shredded Romano cheese, for topping

INSTRUCTIONS

1. In a hot skillet, brown the sausage and bacon, breaking up the sausage as it cooks; drain.

2. Dump the meat into a 4-quart slow cooker. Add the water, broth, sweet potato, garlic, and onion.

3. Cover and cook on low 6 hours (high, 3 hours), until the veggies are tender.

4. Add the kale and cream and season with salt and black pepper.

5. Leave the lid off and cook 15 minutes longer or until heated through and kale is wilted.

6. Top each serving with cheese.

Meatballs & Tortellini Soup

> *Makes about 15 cups*

INGREDIENTS

2 teaspoons each dried basil and
   dried oregano

1 onion, finely chopped

1 cup carrots, shredded

1 tablespoon tomato paste

2 cloves minced garlic

2 tablespoons olive oil

1 red bell pepper, diced

1 (26 ounce) package cooked frozen
   Italian meatballs

1 (14.5 ounce) can petite diced
   tomatoes (don't drain)

1 (15 ounce) can tomato sauce

1 (19 ounce) package frozen
   cheese tortellini

5 teaspoons beef bouillon granules

5 cups water

1 zucchini, diced

Salt and black pepper, to taste

Shredded mozzarella cheese,
   for topping

INGREDIENTS

1. In a microwave-safe bowl, mix the basil, oregano, onion, carrots, tomato paste, garlic, and olive oil.

2. Microwave on high 5 minutes, stirring every 1½ minutes.

3. Transfer the mixture to a 6-quart slow cooker.

4. Add the red bell pepper, cooked frozen Italian meatballs, diced tomatoes, tomato sauce, frozen cheese tortellini, beef bouillon granules, and water.

5. Cover and cook on low 6 hours (high, 3 hours).

6. Stir in the zucchini and season with salt and black pepper. Cook 20 minutes longer.

7. Top each serving with the cheese.

Thai Pork Stew

> *Makes about 8 cups*

INGREDIENTS

2 pounds boneless pork loin, cut into bite-size pieces

2 cups red bell peppers, julienned

2 cups beef stock

¼ cup teriyaki sauce

2 tablespoons rice wine vinegar

1 teaspoon red pepper flakes

2 cloves minced garlic

½ teaspoon salt

1 cup uncooked instant rice

1 (14 ounce) can coconut milk

1 (7 ounce) jar baby corn, drained

¼ cup creamy peanut butter

Sliced green onions, for topping

Peanuts, for topping

INSTRUCTIONS

1. In a 3-quart slow cooker, mix the pork loin, red bell peppers, beef stock, teriyaki sauce, rice wine vinegar, red pepper flakes, garlic, and salt.

2. Cover and cook on low 7 hours (high, 3½ hours).

3. Stir in the rice and coconut milk; cook on low for 20 minutes, until rice is tender.

4. Add the baby corn and peanut butter; stir until peanut butter is melted.

5. Top each serving with green onions and peanuts.

Summer Pesto Soup

> *Makes about 17 cups*

INGREDIENTS

5 cups Yukon gold potatoes, diced

1½ cups baby carrots, halved

1 cup leeks (white and light green parts), diced

2 cups fresh green beans, trimmed and sliced

2 yellow or red tomatoes, diced

1 tablespoon fresh basil, chopped

1 tablespoon oregano, chopped

8 cups water

2 zucchini, cut in half lengthwise and sliced

1 cup frozen lima beans

1 (15.25 ounce) can whole kernel corn, drained

⅔ cup uncooked orzo

⅓ cup prepared basil pesto

Salt and black pepper, to taste

Shredded Parmesan cheese, for topping

vegetarian

INSTRUCTIONS

1. Put the potatoes, carrots, leeks, green beans, tomatoes, basil, oregano, and water into a 5-quart slow cooker.

2. Cover and cook on high 4 hours, until the potatoes are tender.

3. Add the zucchini, lima beans, corn, and orzo. Cover and cook 30 minutes longer or until everything is tender.

4. Stir in the pesto, and season with plenty of salt and black pepper.

5. Top each serving with some cheese.

Taste of Tuscany Chicken Soup

> *Makes about 6 cups*

INGREDIENTS

1 cup onion, chopped

2 tablespoons tomato paste

1 teaspoon salt

1 teaspoon black pepper

1 (15 ounce) can cannellini beans, drained and rinsed

1 (14 ounce) can chicken broth

½ (10 ounce) jar roasted red peppers, drained and chopped

1 pound boneless, skinless chicken thighs, diced

3 cloves garlic, finely chopped

½ teaspoon dried rosemary, crushed

1 (6 ounce) package fresh baby spinach

Shredded Parmesan cheese, for serving

INSTRUCTIONS

1. Toss the onion, tomato paste, salt, black pepper, beans, broth, roasted peppers, chicken, garlic, and rosemary into a 3-quart slow cooker. Cover and cook on high 1 hour.

2. Reduce the heat to low and cook 3 hours longer.

3. Stir in the spinach, cover, and cook about 10 minutes, just until the spinach wilts.

4. Top each serving with cheese.

Also known as white Italian kidney beans, it is said that cannellini beans can provide hours of energy, help stave off cravings, AND control mood swings. Need I say more?

Delicious Duo:

Pair this with Taste of Tuscany Chicken Soup!

Veg-Out Sandwiches

> *Serves* 4

vegetarian

INGREDIENTS

1 carrot, thinly sliced
1 bell pepper, thinly sliced
1 cucumber, thinly sliced
1 tomato, thinly sliced
1 avocado, thinly sliced
4 slices bread
Spinach dip, as needed
Alfalfa sprouts, as needed

INSTRUCTIONS

1. Spread a thick layer of the spinach dip onto four slices of your favorite bread.

2. Pile the veggies on two of the slices and add a nice layer of baby spinach and a handful of alfalfa sprouts.

3. Top with the remaining bread slices; cut and share.

Eastern Clam Chowder

> *Makes about 7 cups*

INGREDIENTS

1 (6.5 ounce) can chopped clams
(don't drain)

1 (10 ounce) can whole baby clams
(don't drain)

¼ pound bacon, cooked
and crumbled

1 small white onion, chopped

4 small white potatoes, peeled
and diced

1¾ teaspoons salt

⅛ teaspoon black pepper

1½ cups water

2 cups half-and-half, divided

2 tablespoons cornstarch

INSTRUCTIONS

1. In a 3-quart slow cooker, combine the chopped clams, whole baby clams, bacon, onion, white potatoes, salt, black pepper, and water.

2. Cover and cook on high 3 hours.

3. Whisk together 1 cup of the half-and-half and cornstarch until well blended, then stir into the cooker and cook 1 hour longer.

4. Stir in remaining 1 cup half-and-half and let stand until heated through.

5. Serve and enjoy!

Split Pea & Smoked Turkey Soup

> *Makes about 8 cups*

INGREDIENTS

10 fresh parsley stems

4 fresh thyme sprigs

1 pound dry green split peas, picked over and rinsed

1 large leek (white and light green parts), halved lengthwise and thinly sliced

2 celery ribs, chopped

2 carrots, chopped

1 teaspoon salt, plus more to taste

½ teaspoon black pepper, plus more to taste

1 large smoked turkey leg

7 cups water

½ cup fresh parsley, chopped

INSTRUCTIONS

1. Use kitchen string to tie together parsley stems and thyme sprigs; toss them into a big oval slow cooker.

2. Stir in the green split peas, leek, celery ribs, carrots, salt, and black pepper.

3. Add the turkey leg and water. Cover and cook on low for 6 to 8 hours, until peas are tender.

4. Remove and discard the herb bundle. Remove the turkey leg; discard the skin and bones, and shred the meat.

5. Whisk the soup to break up some of the peas, stir in parsley and the shredded meat, and season with more salt and black pepper. Serve and enjoy!

Hot & Sour Soup

> *Makes about 14 cups*

INGREDIENTS

1 (8 ounce) package fresh button or shiitake mushrooms, sliced

½ (12 ounce) package broccoli slaw mix

1 (8 ounce) can sliced bamboo shoots, drained and rinsed

1 (12 ounce) package extra-firm water-packed tofu

4⅓ cups water, divided

4 cups vegetable stock

½ cup soy sauce, plus more, to taste

½ tablespoon sriracha hot sauce

1 tablespoon ground ginger

3 tablespoons cornstarch

1 tablespoon toasted sesame oil

1 (9 ounce) package frozen sugar snap peas

1 (8 ounce) package rice noodles

1 teaspoon ground white pepper

¼ cup apple cider vinegar

¼ cup red wine vinegar

Green onions, sliced, for topping

Jalapeño peppers, sliced, for topping

INSTRUCTIONS

1. Pour the mushrooms in an even layer in a 4-quart slow cooker.

2. Top with the broccoli slaw and bamboo shoots.

3. Drain and dice the tofu and toss into the cooker. Add 4 cups water, the stock, soy sauce, hot sauce, and ginger and stir until well blended.

4. Cover and cook on low 8 hours (high, 4 hours).

5. Whisk together the cornstarch, oil, and the remaining ⅓ cup water until lump-free. Slowly stir the mixture into the cooker, cover, and cook for 20 minutes.

6. Stir in the snap peas and noodles; cover and cook 10 minutes longer, then stir in the white pepper and both vinegars. Taste and adjust seasonings if necessary.

7. Top each serving with the green onions and jalapeños.

Delicious Duo:

**Pair this with
Hot & Sour Soup!**

Teriyaki Pork Wraps

> *Serves 8*

INGREDIENTS

1 pound tenderized, boneless pork
   loin chops, cut into ½-inch-
   thick slices

1 tablespoon canola oil

½ cup teriyaki sauce

3 cloves minced garlic

1 teaspoon onion powder

4 (8 inch) flour tortillas, warmed

Romaine lettuce, shredded,
   as needed

Mandarin orange slices, as needed

French-fried onions, as needed

INSTRUCTIONS

1. Trim the pork loin chops and brown in hot canola oil in a
skillet until cooked through.

2. Stir in the teriyaki sauce, garlic, and onion powder; cook
3 minutes, stirring often.

3. Divide the mixture off-center among flour tortillas; top with
the shredded romaine lettuce, mandarin orange slices, and
French-fried onions.

4. Fold, cut in half, and share.

Classic Chicken Noodle Soup

> *Makes about 12 cups*

INGREDIENTS

1 onion, sliced

2 carrots, sliced

2 celery ribs, sliced

4 ounces fresh mushrooms, sliced

1 pound boneless, skinless chicken breast, cut into bite-size pieces

2 teaspoons salt

½ teaspoon black pepper

¼ teaspoon dried thyme

1 tablespoon dried parsley

5 cups water

2 chicken bouillon cubes

3 cups uncooked thin egg noodles

1 cup frozen peas, thawed

INSTRUCTIONS

1. Pour the onion, carrots, celery, mushrooms, and chicken into a 4-quart slow cooker.

2. Sprinkle with the salt, black pepper, thyme, and parsley. Pour the water over the top and toss in the bouillon cubes.

3. Cover and cook on low 8 hours (high, 4 hours).

4. Stir in the noodles, cover, and cook on high 45 minutes longer or until noodles are tender.

5. Stir in the peas and serve.

Loaded Vegetable Soup

> *Makes about 16 cups*

vegetarian

INGREDIENTS

1 onion, diced

1 (16 ounce) package frozen mixed vegetables

1 (15 ounce) can lima beans, drained and rinsed

2 cups frozen sweet corn

1 (16 ounce) package frozen carrots

2 (28 ounce) cans petite diced tomatoes (don't drain)

2 cups frozen okra

2 cups water

2 to 3 teaspoons salt-free seasoning (such as Mrs. Dash Table Blend)

INSTRUCTIONS

1. In a 5-quart slow cooker, pour the onion, frozen mixed vegetables, lima beans, frozen sweet corn, frozen carrots, diced tomatoes, and frozen okra.

2. Stir in the water and salt-free seasoning.

3. Cover and cook on low for 4 hours.

4. Serve and enjoy!

Bacon Cheeseburger Bowls

> *Makes about 10 cups*

INGREDIENTS

1 pound ground beef

1 cup diced onion

1 (14.5 ounce) can diced tomatoes (don't drain)

5 bacon strips, cooked and crumbled

½ cup celery, chopped

1 cup carrots, shredded

2 cups potatoes, peeled and diced

1 (8 ounce) package cream cheese, diced

4 cups chicken broth

2 teaspoons minced garlic

1 teaspoon salt

½ teaspoon black pepper

1½ teaspoons seasoned salt

¼ cup flour

1 cup milk

2 cups shredded sharp cheddar cheese, plus more for topping

Dill pickles, chopped, for serving

INSTRUCTIONS

1. Brown the ground beef with onion in a skillet over medium heat, breaking up the meat as it cooks; drain and pour into a 3-quart slow cooker.

2. Stir in the diced tomatoes, bacon, celery, carrots, potatoes, cream cheese, chicken broth, garlic, salt, black pepper, and seasoned salt.

3. Cover and cook on low 8 hours (high, 4 hours), until the veggies are tender.

4. Whisk together the flour and milk until smooth; slowly stir into the cooker.

5. Stir in the cheddar cheese. Cook uncovered for 10 minutes, until the cheese melts.

6. Top each serving with more cheese and the chopped dill pickles.

Chicken Enchilada Soup

> *Makes about 12 cups*

INGREDIENTS

1 pound boneless, skinless chicken breasts

1 (15.2 ounce) can whole kernel corn, drained

1 (14.5 ounce) can diced tomatoes (don't drain)

1 (14.5 ounce) can chicken broth

1 (10 ounce) can enchilada sauce

1 (4 ounce) can diced green chiles

1 onion, chopped

1½ teaspoons minced garlic

1½ teaspoons chili powder

Salt and black pepper, to taste

¼ cup fresh cilantro, chopped

INSTRUCTIONS

1. Coat a 4-quart slow cooker with cooking spray. Place the chicken in cooker.

2. Add the corn, tomatoes, chicken broth, enchilada sauce, green chiles, onion, garlic, chili powder, salt, black pepper, and cilantro; stir to blend.

3. Cover and cook on low for 5 hours or until the chicken is cooked through.

4. Transfer the chicken to a cutting board and shred meat.

5. Return the shredded meat to cooker; cover and cook 30 minutes to 1 hour more. Serve and enjoy!

TIP: Set out bowls of chopped green onions, diced avocados, chopped fresh cilantro, and shredded cheddar cheese, letting everyone personalize their own soup.

Chicken Tortellini Soup

> *Makes 12 cups*

INGREDIENTS

1 pound boneless, skinless chicken breasts

1 cup carrots, sliced

1 cup celery, sliced

1 cup onion, chopped

2 teaspoons minced garlic

1½ teaspoons salt

1½ teaspoons dried basil

½ teaspoon dried oregano

½ teaspoon cayenne pepper

1 (14.5 ounce) can chicken broth

3½ cups water

2 cups frozen cheese tortellini, thawed

1 cup fresh baby spinach

1 (12 ounce) can evaporated milk

Black pepper, coarsely ground, for garnish

Parmesan cheese, shaved, for garnish

Delicious Duo: Pair this with Cooker Cornbread on page 88!

INSTRUCTIONS

1. Cut the chicken into bite-size pieces and place in a 6-quart slow cooker.

2. Add the carrots, celery, and onion.

3. In a large bowl, stir together the garlic, salt, basil, oregano, cayenne pepper, chicken broth, and water. Pour over the chicken and vegetables in slow cooker.

4. Cover and cook on low for 8 hours.

5. Stir in the tortellini. Turn cooker to high, cover, and cook 30 minutes more or until the tortellini is tender.

6. Turn off cooker; stir in the spinach and evaporated milk. Let set until the spinach is wilted.

7. Coarse black pepper and Parmesan cheese are all that's needed to garnish this simple soup. Serve with Cooker Cornbread and enjoy!.

Homestyle Chili

> *Makes 15 cups*

INGREDIENTS

2 pounds lean ground beef

1 cup celery, sliced

½ cup each red, green, and yellow
  bell pepper, chopped

1 onion, chopped

2 (15 ounce) cans kidney beans
  (drain 1 can)

2 (14.5 ounce) cans diced tomatoes

1 (6 ounce) can tomato paste

2 teaspoons salt

2 teaspoons chili powder

2 teaspoons minced garlic

1 (10.7 ounce) can tomato soup

½ to 1 cup spicy tomato juice

Shredded lettuce, for topping

Shredded cheese, for topping

Black olives, sliced, for topping

Sour cream, for topping

INSTRUCTIONS

1. Crumble the ground beef into a 6-quart slow cooker.

2. Add the celery, bell peppers, onion, kidney beans with remaining juice, tomatoes with juice, tomato paste, salt, chili powder, garlic, soup, and tomato juice. Stir to blend.

3. Cover and cook on low for 6 to 8 hours or until hot and bubbly and the ground beef is cooked through.

4. Serve, topping with the shredded lettuce and cheese, sliced black olives, and sour cream (and anything else you can dream up).

Breakfast

Slow cooker meals aren't just for savory dinners and soups! These breakfast recipes show that you can use your slow cooker to pop food in overnight to wake up to sweet aromas, or rise early to prepare a breakfast of champions.

Overnight Apple Pie Oatmeal

> *Serves 4*

vegetarian

INGREDIENTS

Coconut oil as needed, plus
   1 tablespoon

2 Gala apples

1½ cups coconut milk, plus more
   for serving

1½ cups water

1 cup steel-cut oats

¼ to ½ teaspoon sea salt

1 teaspoon vanilla

Brown sugar, cinnamon, half-and-
   half, honey, maple syrup, chopped
   walnuts, and toasted coconut,
   for serving

INSTRUCTIONS

1. Coat a large slow cooker heavily with coconut oil.

2. Core and dice apples and toss them into the cooker.

3. Add coconut milk, water, steel-cut oats, coconut oil, sea salt, and vanilla. Stir to blend.

4. Cook 5 to 7 hours on low, until the apples and oats are tender.

5. Top servings with brown sugar, cinnamon, half-and-half or coconut milk, honey, and/or maple syrup, and a sprinkling of chopped walnuts and/or toasted coconut.

Coffee Cake Surprise

> *Serves about 8*

INGREDIENTS

¾ cup caramel topping

¼ cup plus 2 tablespoons brown sugar

¾ teaspoon ground cinnamon

6 tablespoons plus 2¼ cups biscuit baking mix, divided

1 cup plus 2 tablespoons sugar

¾ cup sour cream or vanilla yogurt

1 egg, lightly beaten

1 egg yolk, lightly beaten

1½ teaspoon vanilla extract

TIP: The jar in the center not only gives your cake "bundt appeal," but you can fill it with other toppings, like jam or honey.

vegetarian

INSTRUCTIONS

1. Coat a 4-quart slow cooker with cooking spray and line with parchment paper.

2. Pour caramel topping into an 8-ounce canning jar. Place lid and ring on jar, but do not tighten completely; set jar in the center of cooker. Coat jar and paper with cooking spray.

3. In a medium bowl, stir together brown sugar, cinnamon, and 6 tablespoons baking mix.

4. In a large bowl, stir together remaining 2¼ cups baking mix, sugar, sour cream, egg, egg yolk, and vanilla until well blended.

5. Spread half the batter around jar in cooker. Sprinkle with half the set-aside streusel mixture; repeat layers.

6. Place a double layer of paper towels over opening in cooker, making sure towels extend beyond the opening.

7. Cover and cook on high for 1¾ to 2¼ hours or until a toothpick inserted halfway between jar and side of cooker comes out clean.

8. Uncover, remove insert from cooker, and let set for 10 minutes. Using a potholder, carefully remove jar from insert by twisting and lifting.

9. Remove coffee cake from insert by lifting parchment paper. Drizzle hot caramel over cake.

Blueberry French Toast

> *Serves* about 8

INGREDIENTS

8 eggs

½ cup plain yogurt

⅓ cup sour cream

1 teaspoon vanilla extract

½ teaspoon ground cinnamon

¼ cup brown sugar

1 cup milk

⅓ cup pure maple syrup

1 (1 pound) loaf French bread, cubed

1½ cup fresh blueberries, plus more
    for serving

12 ounces cream cheese, cubed

Powdered sugar, as needed

Syrup, as needed

vegetarian

INSTRUCTIONS

1. Coat a 6-quart slow cooker with cooking spray.

2. In a large bowl, whisk together the eggs, yogurt, sour cream, vanilla, cinnamon, and brown sugar until well beaten. Gradually whisk in the milk and syrup until blended; set aside.

3. Place half the bread in prepared cooker, followed by half each of the berries, cream cheese, and egg mixture. Repeat layers.

4. Cover and refrigerate overnight. Remove from refrigerator 30 minutes before cooking. Then, cover and cook on low for 3 to 4 hours or until eggs are cooked through.

5. Just add a dusting of powdered sugar, your favorite syrup, and extra berries, if you'd like. What a yummy way to start your day!

Sausage & Egg "Bake"

> *Serves* about 12

INGREDIENTS

1 (9.6 ounce) package fully cooked frozen sausage links, thawed

1 (1 pound, 14 ounce) package frozen shredded hash browns, thawed

2 cups shredded mozzarella cheese

½ cup grated Parmesan cheese

¼ cup sun-dried tomatoes in oil, drained and chopped

¾ cup green onions, sliced

12 eggs

½ cup milk

1 teaspoon dry mustard

Salt, to taste

TIP: This tastes just as delicious if you substitute 2 cups of fully cooked chopped ham for the sausage and 2 cups of shredded cheddar for the mozzarella!

INSTRUCTIONS

1. Slice the sausage links.

2. Coat a 6-quart slow cooker with cooking spray.

3. Place half the hash browns in an even layer in cooker. Top with half each of the sausage slices, mozzarella, Parmesan, sun dried tomatoes, and green onions. Repeat layers; set aside.

4. In a medium bowl, whisk together the eggs, milk, dry mustard, and salt until well blended. Pour evenly over layers in cooker.

5. Cover and cook on high for 3 hours or until the eggs are cooked through. Serve and enjoy!

Huevos Rancheros

> *Serves 8*

vegetarian

INGREDIENTS

1 tablespoon butter

10 eggs, beaten

1 cup half-and-half

1 (8 ounce) package shredded
   Mexican cheese blend

½ teaspoon black pepper

½ teaspoon minced garlic

¼ teaspoon chili powder

1 (4 ounce) can diced green chiles

8 (6 inch) corn tortillas

1 to 2 tablespoons olive oil

INSTRUCTIONS

1. Grease a 2-quart slow cooker with butter, leaving any remaining butter in cooker.

2. In a large bowl, whisk together the eggs and half-and-half until well blended. Stir in the Mexican cheese, black pepper, garlic, chili powder, and chiles. Pour into prepared cooker.

3. Cover and cook on low for 3½ hours. Then turn off cooker.

4. Heat oil over medium-high heat in a skillet. Fry the tortillas, one at a time, until lightly browned and bubbly; drain on paper towels and cover with foil to keep warm.

5. Serve eggs on the tortillas. Add on the chopped tomato, jalapeño, or green bell pepper; refried or black beans; enchilada or haut sauce; lettuce or arugula … the options are endless.

Sides
& Snacks

The recipes in this section taste just as good on their own as they do with a main dish. Feel free to mix and match these recipes with the mains starting on page 90, or use them to complement another dish that needs an extra slow-cooked touch of scrumptious.

Loaded Potatoes

> *Serves 10 to 12*

INGREDIENTS

10 to 12 red potatoes, thinly sliced

Salt and black pepper, to taste

1 teaspoon garlic salt

½ pound bacon strips, cooked
   and crumbled

1 onion, finely chopped

1 (8 ounce) package shredded sharp
   cheddar cheese

¼ cup butter, cut into small pieces

INSTRUCTIONS

1. Line a 6-quart slow cooker with foil; coat foil with cooking spray.

2. Arrange half the potatoes in cooker; sprinkle with salt and black pepper.

3. Add half each of the garlic salt, bacon, onion, cheddar, and butter. Repeat layers.

4. Cover and cook on low for 7 to 8 hours or until potatoes are tender.

Slow Cooker Baked Potatoes

Wrap russet potatoes in foil and arrange in a slow cooker. Cover and cook on low about 6 hours or until potatoes are tender; unwrap and split. Add your favorite yummy toppings.

Bacon-Wrapped Corn

> *Serves 6*

INGREDIENTS

6 tablespoons butter, softened

2 teaspoons minced garlic

½ teaspoon each salt and dried dill weed

1 teaspoon coarse black pepper

12 mini ears frozen sweet corn, thawed

12 bacon strips, partially cooked

½ cup chicken broth

1 red bell pepper, chopped

TIP: Partially cooked bacon is still easily wrapped around the corn chunks. If it is cooked to the crisp stage, wrapping will be very difficult. Bacon will finish cooking in the slow cooker.

Delicious Duo: Pair this with Chicken Cordon Bleu on page 98!

INSTRUCTIONS

1. In a small bowl, stir together the butter, garlic, salt, dill weed, and black pepper.

2. Spread about 1½ teaspoons of the butter mixture over each chunk of corn; wrap each with a bacon strip, pressing edges to seal or securing with toothpicks.

3. Place as many chunks as possible in a single layer in a 6-quart slow cooker; stack any remaining chunks on top.

4. Add the chicken broth and bell pepper. Cover and cook on low for 3 to 3½ hours or until corn is tender.

Creamy Loaded Corn

> *Serves about 12*

INGREDIENTS

1½ cups half-and-half

1 cup onion, chopped

48 ounces frozen whole kernel corn, thawed, divided

¼ cup butter, cubed

1 teaspoon sugar

½ teaspoon each salt and black pepper

1 tablespoon canola oil

2 cups shredded Pepper Jack cheese, divided

¼ pound bacon, cooked and crumbled

INSTRUCTIONS

1. Coat a 4-quart slow cooker with cooking spray.

2. In a blender, combine half-and-half, onion, and about 2½ cups corn. Cover and blend until nearly smooth. Pour into prepared cooker.

3. Stir in remaining corn, butter, sugar, salt, black pepper, oil, ½ cup Pepper Jack, and bacon.

4. Cover and cook on low about 3 hours or until corn is hot.

5. Sprinkle remaining 1½ cups Pepper Jack over corn mixture; stir.

6. Cover and continue cooking 30 minutes more or until cheese is melted.

TIP: Crumbled bacon and a handful of chopped chives to give this corn a pop of color and an even bigger boost of flavor.

Fruited Rice Pilaf

❯ *Serves 10 to 15*

INGREDIENTS

1 cup each uncooked wild rice and brown rice, rinsed

2 tablespoons butter, melted

1 (32 ounce) carton chicken broth

1 cup sweet onion, diced

½ teaspoon black pepper

Zest and juice from 1 orange

1 (5.5 ounce) package dried sweetened cherries

1 cup toasted pecans, toasted and chopped

INSTRUCTIONS

1. Coat a 4-quart slow cooker with cooking spray. In cooker, stir together the wild rice, brown rice, and butter.

2. Stir in the chicken broth, onion, black pepper, and orange zest.

3. Cover and cook on high for 3 to 4 hours or until rice is tender. Add cherries and fluff with a fork.

4. Turn off cooker, cover, and let set for 15 minutes.

5. To toast pecans, place them in a single layer in a dry skillet over medium heat for approximately 6 minutes or until golden brown.

5. Stir the toasted pecans into rice and drizzle orange juice over the top.

Rice Recreated

Mix 4 cups leftover pilaf, 1 egg, 1 tablespoon grated Parmesan cheese, and 2 cups breadcrumbs; form patties and fry in hot oil until heated through. Eat plain or serve on a bun with provolone cheese.

Cooker Cornbread

> *Serves 8*

INGREDIENTS

1¼ cups flour

¾ cup yellow cornmeal

¼ cup sugar

1 tablespoon plus 1½ teaspoon
    baking powder

1 teaspoon salt

1 egg, lightly beaten

¾ cup heavy cream

⅓ cup butter, melted

¼ cup water

Butter, for serving

Jam, for serving

Honey, for serving

Delicious Duo:

Pair this with Chicken Tortellini Soup on page 72!

vegetarian

INSTRUCTIONS

1. Heavily coat a 2-quart slow cooker with cooking spray.

2. In a medium bowl, combine the flour, cornmeal, sugar, baking powder, and salt; stir lightly. Add egg, cream, butter, and ¼ cup water. Stir until just moistened. Spread evenly in prepared cooker.

3. Cover and cook on high for 2 to 3 hours, or until a toothpick inserted in center comes out nearly clean. Remove insert from cooker, uncover, and set on a wire rack to cool.

4. Carefully invert cooker and turn cornbread out onto a cutting board or wire rack.

5. Let the bread cool slightly before cutting. Then serve with butter and jam or honey, or alongside soup or chili.

Green Beans Alfredo

> *Serves about 10*

INGREDIENTS

- 2 (16 ounce) packages frozen French-cut green beans, thawed
- 1 (15 ounce) jar alfredo sauce
- 1 (8 ounce) can water chestnuts, drained and diced
- 1 (4 ounce) can sliced mushrooms, drained
- ¼ cup roasted red peppers, chopped
- ⅓ cup Parmesan cheese, grated
- ½ teaspoon black pepper
- 1 (6 ounce) container French-fried onions, divided

Delicious Duo:

Pair this with Italian Beef on page 104!

vegetarian

INGREDIENTS

1. Coat a 4-quart slow cooker with cooking spray.

2. In a large bowl, stir together the green beans, alfredo sauce, water chestnuts, mushrooms, red peppers, Parmesan, black pepper, and half the French-fried onions. Pour into prepared cooker.

3. Cover and cook on low for 4½ hours or until hot and bubbly.

4. Top with the remaining French-fried onions before serving.

Mains

Now, for the main event: entrées that can be slow cooked
to perfection! Whether you prepare these recipes for lunch
or dinner, you will find flavorful, bold tastes—and discover
just how easy it really is to make meals in the slow cooker.

Easy Slow Cooker French Dip

❯ *Serves 6*

INGREDIENTS

4 pounds rump roast

1 (10 ½ ounce) can beef broth

1 (10½ oz.) can condensed French onion soup

1 (12 ounce) can or bottle beer

6 French rolls

2 tablespoons butter

Provolone cheese, for serving

INSTRUCTIONS

1. Trim excess fat from the rump roast and place in a slow cooker.

2. Add the beef broth, onion soup, and beer. Cook on low setting for 7 hours.

3. Preheat oven to 350°F.

4. Split the French rolls and spread with butter. Bake 10 minutes or until heated through.

5. Slice the meat on the diagonal and place on the rolls. Add provolone cheese on top of the meat. Serve the sauce for dipping.

Chili Orange Chicken

> *Serves 4*

INGREDIENTS

¾ cup enchilada sauce

¼ cup BBQ sauce

1 teaspoon salt, divided

1 tablespoon chili powder

1 teaspoon ground cumin

4 bone-in skin-on chicken
   breast halves

⅓ cup orange marmalade

½ cup chopped cilantro

1 tablespoon orange zest

INSTRUCTIONS

1. In a large greased slow cooker, mix the enchilada sauce, BBQ sauce, and ½ teaspoon of the salt.

2. On a plate, mix the chili powder, cumin, and remaining ½ teaspoon salt. Coat the chicken with the dry mixture and arrange in the cooker.

3. Cover and cook on high for 2½ to 3 hours, until the internal temperature of the chicken reaches 165°F.

4. Turn off the cooker; transfer the chicken to a serving plate.

5. To the liquid in the cooker, stir in the marmalade, cilantro, and orange zest and serve over the chicken.

Saucy Meatballs

> *Serves 8 to 10*

INGREDIENTS

1 (28 ounce) can crushed tomatoes

½ cup beef broth

1 (6 ounce) can tomato paste

1 tablespoon sugar

1 onion, chopped

1½ teaspoons minced garlic

Salt and red pepper flakes, to taste

1 pound each lean ground beef and
    ground pork

⅓ cup Italian breadcrumbs

1 egg

¼ cup milk

¼ cup grated Parmesan cheese

Cooked spaghett, for serving

INSTRUCTIONS

1. In a 4-quart slow cooker, stir together the tomatoes with juice, beef broth, tomato paste, sugar, onion, garlic, salt, and red pepper flakes.

2. In a large bowl, mix the ground beef, ground pork, breadcrumbs, egg, milk, Parmesan, and more salt and red pepper flakes.

3. Using a rounded tablespoonful, shape mixture into 30 balls; place in cooker and submerge in sauce.

4. Cover and cook on low for 5 to 6 hours or until meatballs are cooked through. Skim grease from sauce before serving with spaghetti.

TIP: Place meatballs and a little sauce on French rolls; top with shredded mozzarella.

Vegetable Lasagna

> *Serves about 8*

vegetarian

INGREDIENTS

1 egg

1 (15 ounce) tub ricotta cheese

1 (6 ounce) package baby spinach, coarsely chopped

3 portobello mushroom caps, gills removed and thinly sliced

1 zucchini, thinly sliced

1 (28 ounce) can crushed tomatoes

2 (14.5 ounce) cans diced fire-roasted tomatoes

2 teaspoon minced garlic

1½ teaspoons each Italian seasoning and salt

½ teaspoon black pepper

15 uncooked whole wheat lasagna noodles

3½ cups shredded mozzarella cheese, divided

INSTRUCTIONS

1. Coat a 6-quart slow cooker with cooking spray.

2. In a large bowl, stir together the egg, ricotta, spinach, mushrooms, and zucchini; set aside.

3. In a medium bowl, stir together all tomatoes with juice, garlic, Italian seasoning, salt, and black pepper.

4. Spread 1½ cups tomato mixture in prepared cooker.

5. Arrange five noodles over tomato mixture in cooker, overlapping and breaking as needed to cover tomatoes. Spread half the ricotta mixture over the noodles and pat down firmly. Cover with 1½ cups tomato mixture and 1 cup mozzarella. Repeat layers.

6. Arrange five noodles over the top, overlapping and breaking as needed; cover with remaining tomato mixture.

7. Cover and cook on low for 4 to 5 hours or until noodles are tender.

8. Turn off cooker and sprinkle remaining 1½ cups mozzarella over lasagna.

9. Cover and let stand for 15 to 20 minutes or until cheese is melted. Serve and enjoy!

For Meat Lovers

Replace mushrooms with 1 pound cooked and drained ground beef, adding onion if desired. Slow cook as directed.

Chicken Cordon Bleu

➤ *Serves 6*

INGREDIENTS

1 (10.7 ounce) can cream of
  chicken soup

2 teaspoons minced garlic

1 teaspoon seasoned salt

½ teaspoon black pepper

½ cup milk

4 to 6 small boneless, skinless
  chicken breast halves

6 slices deli ham

6 slices Swiss cheese

1 (6 ounce) package chicken-flavored
  stuffing mix

¼ cup butter, melted

INSTRUCTIONS

1. Coat a 7-quart slow cooker with cooking spray.

2. In a medium bowl, whisk together the soup, garlic, seasoned salt, black pepper, and milk until well combined. Pour enough soup mixture into cooker to just cover the bottom.

3. Arrange the chicken in cooker and spread a little soup mixture over chicken. Cover each breast half with one slice each ham and Swiss. Pour the remaining soup mixture over the top.

4. Cover and cook on low for 5 hours; then, sprinkle with the stuffing mix and drizzle with butter.

5. Cover and cook 1 hour more or until the chicken is cooked through.

Try It Rolled!

Flatten chicken breast halves to ½-inch thickness. Place one slice each ham and Swiss on each breast half and roll up, securing with toothpicks; arrange in cooker. Cook as directed above.

Delicious Duo:

Pair this with Bacon-Wrapped Corn on page 85!

Jambalaya

> *Serves 12*

INGREDIENTS

4 chicken thighs

1 pound smoked sausage

1 each red and green bell pepper

1 jalapeño pepper (optional)

2 to 3 canned chipotle peppers in adobo sauce

1 onion

½ cup celery, sliced

1 (14.5 ounce) can diced tomatoes

1 (6 ounce) can tomato paste

1¾ cups beef stock

2½ teaspoons minced garlic

1 tablespoon dried parsley

1½ teaspoons salt

1½ teaspoons cayenne pepper

½ pound shrimp, peeled and deveined

1½ cups quick-cooking rice

Cajun seasoning, to taste

INSTRUCTIONS

1. Coat a 4-quart slow cooker with cooking spray.

2. Remove skin and bones from the chicken thighs; cut into bite-size pieces and place in prepared cooker. Slice the sausage and add to cooker.

3. Chop the bell peppers, jalapeño pepper (if using), chipotle peppers, and onion; place in a bowl. Stir in celery, tomatoes with juice, tomato paste, beef stock, garlic, parsley, salt, and cayenne pepper. Pour over meat in cooker.

4. Cover and cook on high for 3½ hours.

5. Carefully stir in shrimp and rice.

6. Cover and cook 15 to 20 minutes more or until shrimp turn pink and rice is tender. Stir in the Cajun seasoning, if desired.

Jambalaya-Stuffed Peppers

Stuff leftover jambalaya into hollowed-out green bell peppers and bake at 375°F for 20 minutes or until heated through.

Turkey Dinner

> *Serves 6 to 8*

INGREDIENTS

1 (12 ounce) package
  stuffing cubes

½ cup hot water

2 tablespoons butter, softened
  and cut into pieces

1 onion, chopped

1 cup fresh mushrooms, sliced

½ cup dried
  sweetened cranberries

6 carrots, cut into pieces

1 (3 to 3½ pound) boneless
  turkey breast

¼ teaspoon dried basil

½ teaspoon each salt and
  black pepper

INSTRUCTIONS

1. Coat a 6-quart slow cooker with cooking spray. Put the stuffing cubes in cooker and drizzle the hot water over the top.

2. Layer the butter, onion, mushrooms, cranberries, and carrots over stuffing. Set the turkey breast on top and sprinkle with basil, salt, and black pepper.

3. Cover and cook on low for 8 to 9 hours or until turkey is cooked through.

4. Transfer the turkey to a cutting board and cover loosely with foil; set aside.

5. Thoroughly stir the stuffing mixture in cooker and let set for 5 minutes.

6. Slice the turkey and serve with stuffing mixture.

7. Serve with Cran-Orange Bread (recipe on page 103) for a perfect flavor combo.

Delicious Duo:

Pair this with Turkey Dinner!

Cran-Orange Bread

> *Makes 1 loaf*

vegetarian

INGREDIENTS

3 cups flour

1⅓ cups sugar

1 tablespoon baking powder

¼ teaspoon baking soda

¼ teaspoon salt

⅔ cup nonfat dry milk

1 egg, beaten

2 cups hot water

¼ cup canola oil

1 cup dried
    sweetened cranberries

1 tablespoon orange zest

½ cup pecans, chopped

½ cup semisweet chocolate
    chips, chopped

Butter, for serving

Cream cheese, for serving

Orange marmalade, for serving

INSTRUCTIONS

1. Coat a 4-quart slow cooker heavily with cooking spray.

2. In a large mixing bowl, stir together the flour, sugar, baking powder, baking soda, and salt.

3. In a separate bowl, whisk together the dry milk and hot water until dissolved; add to flour mixture.

4. Add the egg and oil; beat on medium speed for 2 minutes. Fold in cranberries, orange zest, pecans, and chocolate chips.

5. Spread evenly in prepared cooker.

6. Cover and cook on high for 2 to 3 hours, checking for doneness occasionally. Bread is done when the top feels firm.

7. Uncover and let set in cooker for 10 minutes before turning out on a wire rack to cool completely.

8. Just add butter, cream cheese, and/or orange marmalade to make this sweet bread the star of your table.

Italian Beef

> *Serves 12 to 15*

INGREDIENTS

4½ to 5 pounds beef roast, such as chuck

1 (12 ounce) jar beef gravy

1 to 2 cups zesty Italian salad dressing

3 tablespoons canola oil

1 onion, sliced

1 green bell pepper, sliced

Salt and black pepper, to taste

12 to 15 sandwich buns

Shredded mozzarella cheese, for topping

INSTRUCTIONS

1. Coat a 6-quart slow cooker with cooking spray. Place the roast in cooker and pour gravy over the top.

2. Cover and cook on low for 7 to 8 hours.

3. Transfer the roast to a cutting board and shred meat. Discard juices from cooker. Return the shredded meat to cooker and add dressing; stir to coat meat.

4. Cover, turn off cooker, and let set for 30 minutes.

5. Meanwhile, in a large skillet over medium-high heat, heat the oil. Add the onion, bell pepper, salt, and black pepper, cooking until crisp-tender.

6. Serve the meat and vegetables on buns; sprinkle each with a little mozzarella.

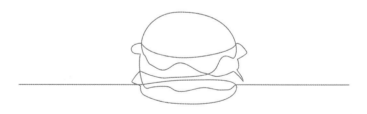

**Pair this with
Green Beans Alfredo
on page 89!**

Teriyaki Pork

> *Serves* about 8

INGREDIENTS

1 (3 to 4 pound) boneless pork roast

1 cup brown sugar

1 onion, sliced and separated
  into rings

⅓ cup pineapple juice

⅓ cup soy sauce

1 teaspoon minced garlic

1 teaspoon ground ginger

Salt and black pepper, to taste

2 tablespoons cornstarch

3 tablespoons cold water

Delicious Idea

After cooking, shred meat and stir into thickened juices. Pile onto buns and top with pineapple and red onion slices.

INSTRUCTIONS

1. Coat a 4-quart slow cooker with cooking spray.

2. Coat the roast with brown sugar and place in prepared cooker; add the onion. Set aside.

3. In a small bowl, stir together the pineapple juice, soy sauce, garlic, and ginger; pour over roast in cooker. Sprinkle with salt and black pepper.

4. Cover and cook on low for 5 to 6 hours or until the roast is cooked to about 135°F; transfer the roast to a bowl.

5. Strain solids from juices, returning juices to cooker and discarding solids; turn cooker to high.

6. In a small bowl, stir together the cornstarch and cold water until smooth. Gradually stir into the juices in cooker. Return the roast to cooker.

7. Cover and cook on high for 45 minutes or until the juices have thickened and roast is cooked through.

8. Slice the roast and serve with thickened gravy.

Buffalo Chicken Pasta

> *Serves about 12*

INGREDIENTS

2 (10.7 ounce) cans cream of
chicken soup

1 cup buffalo wing sauce

1 onion, finely chopped

2½ pounds boneless, skinless
chicken breasts

Salt and black pepper, to taste

Garlic powder, to taste

1½ (16 ounce) packages uncooked
penne pasta

1 (16 ounce) tub sour cream

½ cup ranch salad dressing

1 cup shredded mozzarella cheese

Buffalo Chicken Wraps

Omit pasta. Cook chicken as
directed, but don't add sour cream,
salad dressing, or mozzarella.
Instead, pile chicken mixture
onto flour tortillas; add some
sour cream, salad dressing, and
mozzarella to each.

INSTRUCTIONS

1. Coat a 7-quart slow cooker with cooking spray. Pour both
cans of soup and wing sauce into cooker; add the onion.

2. Cut the chicken into bite-size pieces and season with salt,
black pepper, and garlic powder; add to prepared cooker and
stir to combine.

3. Cover and cook on high for 3 to 4 hours or until the chicken
is cooked through. Turn off cooker.

4. Cook the pasta according to package directions; drain and
add to chicken mixture. Stir in the sour cream, salad dressing,
and mozzarella. Let set a few minutes before serving.

Fiesta Mac & Cheese

> *Serves about 8*

vegetarian

INGREDIENTS

¼ cup butter, melted

1 teaspoon sea salt

½ teaspoon each garlic powder, dry mustard, and black pepper

1 (12 ounce) plus 1 (5 ounce) can evaporated milk

1 (10.7 ounce) can nacho cheese soup

3 cups uncooked rigatoni pasta

2½ cups shredded Mexican cheese blend, divided

1 cup milk

2 tablespoons olive oil

1 cup panko breadcrumbs

Pinch cayenne pepper

TIP: Stir on cooked, chopped bacon. It adds extra crunch and saltiness!

INSTRUCTIONS

1. Coat a 4-quart slow cooker with cooking spray.

2. In cooker, whisk together the butter, salt, garlic powder, dry mustard, black pepper, both cans evaporated milk, and soup.

3. Stir in the pasta and 1 cup of cheese, making sure pasta is submerged.

4. Cover and cook on high for 1½ hours.

5. Stir in the milk and remaining 1½ cups cheese; cover and cook 30 minutes more or until cheese is melted and pasta is tender.

6. In a small saucepan over medium-low heat, heat olive oil. Add the breadcrumbs and cayenne pepper; cook for a few minutes until lightly browned. Sprinkle over the macaroni before serving.

Honey-Apple Pork

> *Serves about 10*

INGREDIENTS

3 tablespoons olive oil

¼ teaspoon each ground nutmeg and ground cloves

½ teaspoon ground cinnamon, plus more for sprinkling

⅓ cup honey, plus more for drizzling

2½ to 3 pounds pork loin

2 Red Delicious apples

INSTRUCTIONS

1. In a large, zippered plastic bag, combine the oil, nutmeg, cloves, cinnamon, and honey.

2. Seal bag and squeeze to mix ingredients.

3. Cut long crosswise slits in the pork loin and place in bag with the honey mixture. Close bag and turn several times to coat the pork. Refrigerate overnight.

4. Coat a 4-quart slow cooker with cooking spray. Thinly slice 1½ apples and arrange in cooker.

5. Remove the pork from bag and place in cooker.

6. Slice remaining ½ apple and push slices into slits in pork. Drizzle with a little honey and sprinkle with a bit of cinnamon.

7. Cook on low for 7 hours or until the pork is cooked through.

Make It a Sandwich

Add buns and slice the pork for sandwiches. Top with BBQ sauce, mayo, banana peppers, or even apple butter.

Beef Brisket in Beer

> *Serves 8*

INGREDIENTS

4 pounds beef brisket

½ teaspoon pepper, plus more
   to taste

1 large onion, sliced and separated
   into rings

½ cup chili sauce

3 tablespoons brown sugar

2 cloves garlic, pressed

¾ cup light beer

3 tablespoons all-purpose flour

INSTRUCTIONS

1. Trim fat from the brisket and cut brisket in half. Sprinkle
with pepper.

2. Place the onion rings in bottom of slow cooker; top
with brisket.

3. Stir together the chili sauce, brown sugar, garlic, and light
beer; pour over brisket. Cover and cook on high for 4 to 6 hours
or on low for 8 to 12 hours.

4. Remove the brisket and set aside, reserving liquid in
slow cooker.

5. Remove 1 cup of the reserved liquid from slow cooker; whisk
in flour and pour into slow cooker, whisking constantly for
5 minutes, or until thickened.

6. Serve over the brisket; sprinkle with pepper.

Slow Cooker Kielbasa & Beer

> *Serves 6 to 8*

INGREDIENTS

2 pounds kielbasa sausage, cut into 1-inch pieces

1 (12 ounce) can or bottle beer

1 (20 ounce) can sauerkraut, drained

Chives, chopped, for topping

INSTRUCTIONS

In a slow cooker, combine sausage, beer, and sauerkraut. Cook on low for 5 to 6 hours until the meat is tender and plump. Season with chives. Serve and enjoy!

Hawaiian Pizza

> *Serves* 4

INGREDIENTS

1 (13.8 ounce) tube refrigerated pizza crust

¾ cup pizza sauce

Salt and black pepper, to taste

1 to 2 cups shredded pizza cheese blend

1 (8 ounce) can pineapple tidbits, well drained

1 cup ham, cubed

⅓ cup green bell pepper or jalapeño pepper, diced

INSTRUCTIONS

1. Line a 7-quart slow cooker with foil; coat foil with cooking spray.

2. Unroll the dough and place in prepared cooker, stretching to cover bottom and 1 inch up sides.

3. Spread the pizza sauce evenly over dough in bottom of cooker. Sprinkle with the salt, black pepper, and pizza cheese. Arrange the pineapple, ham, and bell pepper over cheese.

4. Cover and cook on high for 1¾ to 2¼ hours or until the pizza begins to brown and pull away from foil.

5. Turn off cooker, uncover, and let set for 20 minutes. Remove the pizza from cooker by lifting foil. Serve and enjoy!

Add a Flavor Boost

Cook sliced onions in 1 tablespoon oil for 15 minutes or until caramelized. Add onion to pizza when cover is removed from cooker; let set as directed. Then, scatter baby spinach on top. Yum!

Dessert

The recipes in this section show you how to
make moist cake, delicious brownies, flavorful
cobbler, and even holiday treats—all in a
slow cooker! The cooking may be slow, but
the tastes of these desserts hit you fast.

Pumpkin Dessert

> *Serves about 6*

vegetarian

INGREDIENTS

1 (15 ounce) can pumpkin

2 (5 ounce) cans evaporated milk

2 ounces spiced rum

¾ cup brown sugar

⅔ cup biscuit baking mix, divided

2 eggs, lightly beaten

2 teaspoons pumpkin pie spice

2 tablespoons butter, cut into pieces

¼ cup sugar

Whipped topping, for serving

Nutmeg, as needed, for serving

INSTRUCTIONS

1. Coat a 2-quart slow cooker with cooking spray.

2. In a large bowl, stir together the pumpkin, evaporated milk, rum, brown sugar, 3½ tablespoons baking mix, eggs, and pumpkin pie spice.

3. Pour the mixture into prepared slow cooker. Scatter the butter on top; sprinkle with sugar and remaining baking mix.

4. Cover and cook on low for 6½ to 7½ hours or until mixture is thick and top is golden brown.

5. Just add a dollop of whipped topping and a sprinkle of nutmeg. Served warm or cold, this dessert is just the right ending to your holiday meal or a nice treat any time of year.

Pineapple Upside-Down Cake

> *Serves 8*

vegetarian

INGREDIENTS

¼ cup butter, cut into small pieces, plus more for greasing and ¼ cup, softened

¾ cup brown sugar

3 tablespoons dark rum or pineapple juice

1 (20 ounce) can pineapple slices, juice reserved

8 maraschino cherries

¾ cup cake flour

¾ teaspoon baking powder

½ teaspoon ground cinnamon

¼ teaspoon each ground nutmeg and salt

⅔ cup sugar

1 egg

1 egg yolk

2 tablespoons half-and-half

INSTRUCTIONS

1. Grease a 4-quart slow cooker with butter; line with parchment paper and grease the paper. Turn cooker to high.

2. Scatter the butter pieces in cooker; sprinkle with brown sugar and drizzle with rum.

3. Arrange the pineapple slices over brown sugar, overlapping slightly and pressing gently; place a cherry in the center of each slice. Set aside.

4. In a small bowl, sift together the cake flour, baking powder, cinnamon, nutmeg, and salt.

5. In a medium mixing bowl, beat the sugar and ¼ cup softened butter until light and fluffy. Mix in egg and egg yolk.

6. Slowly add half-and-half, ¼ cup reserved pineapple juice, and flour mixture, beating until well blended and smooth. Pour evenly over the pineapple in cooker.

7. Place a double layer of paper towels over opening in cooker, making sure towels extend beyond the opening, to keep condensation from dripping off the lid and onto the cake.

8. Cover and cook on high for 2 to 2½ hours or until the cake springs back when touched in the center.

9. Turn off cooker and let set for 20 minutes. Use the parchment paper to lift the cake from cooker. Carefully invert cake onto a serving plate. Enjoy!

Deluxe Brownies

> *Serves about 8*

INGREDIENTS

½ cup butter

2 (4 ounce) packages bittersweet
   chocolate, chopped

1 cup sugar

3 eggs, lightly beaten

1¼ cups flour

¼ cup unsweetened cocoa powder

¾ teaspoon baking powder

½ teaspoon sea salt

½ cup chopped walnuts,
   finely chopped

1 cup semisweet chocolate chips

Poswdered sugar, for dusting

vegetarian

INSTRUCTIONS

1. Coat a 4-quart slow cooker with cooking spray; line cooker with parchment paper and coat paper with cooking spray.

2. Melt the butter and chocolate together; stir in the sugar and eggs.

3. Combine the flour, cocoa powder, baking powder, and salt; stir into chocolate mixture. Add the walnuts and chocolate chips, stirring until just moistened. Spread evenly in prepared cooker.

4. Cover and cook on low for 4 hours.

5. Uncover and cook 45 minutes more or until about 1 inch around the outer edges appears done. (Brownies will look undercooked in the center, but will be set up as they cool.)

6. Remove insert from cooker, uncover, and set on a wire rack to cool completely. Remove the brownies from cooker by lifting parchment paper.

7. Dust with a little powdered sugar. No frosting needed. Simple. Delicious. And cooked in a slow cooker. Who would've thought?

Double Berry Cobbler

> *Serves 8*

INGREDIENTS

1¼ cups flour, divided

2 tablespoons plus 1 cup sugar, divided

1 teaspoon baking powder

¼ teaspoon ground cinnamon

1 egg, lightly beaten

¼ cup milk

2 tablespoons canola oil

⅛ teaspoon salt

2 cups fresh raspberries

2 cups fresh blueberries

Ice cream, optional

TIP: Try this recipe using pitted cherries or sliced peaches, nectarines, or apricots. Fruit never tasted so good!

vegetarian

INSTRUCTIONS

1. Coat a 4-quart slow cooker with cooking spray.

2. In a large bowl, stir together 1 cup flour, 2 tablespoons sugar, baking powder, and cinnamon.

3. In a small bowl, whisk together the egg, milk, and oil; add to the flour mixture and stir until just moistened.

4. Spread the batter evenly in prepared cooker. In a large bowl, mix the salt, remaining ¼ cup flour, and remaining 1 cup sugar.

5. Add the raspberries and blueberries; stir until well coated. Scatter evenly over batter in cooker.

6. Cover and cook on high for 2 hours or until the cake portion is done.

7. Serve with ice cream, if you'd like.

Meals for Two

You don't have to be cooking for a large group of people when using a slow cooker. This section takes you through recipes made for just one or two people to enjoy. And don't worry—if you find a recipe that you'd like to share, simply double the ingredients! The more—or less—the merrier.

Apricot Oatmeal

> *Serves 2*

vegetarian

INGREDIENTS

1 cup water

¾ cup steel-cut oats

½ cup dried apricots, chopped

2 tablespoons currants

1 cup evaporated milk or soy milk

1 teaspoon vanilla extract

Ground cinnamon, for topping

INSTRUCTIONS

1. In a 1½-quart slow cooker, combine the water, oats, apricots, currants, evaporated milk, and vanilla; stir well.

2. Cover and cook on low for 8 to 9 hours or until tender and thick.

3. Sprinkle lightly with cinnamon and serve hot with desired toppings.

4. Top with vanilla yogurt, half-and-half, honey, brown sugar, maple syrup, nuts, apricot preserves, or fresh fruit for added flavor.

Hash Brown Casserole

> *Serves 2*

INGREDIENTS

⅓ cup sour cream

⅓ cup from (10.7 ounce) can cream of mushroom soup with roasted garlic

⅓ cup shredded American cheese, plus more for sprinkling

2 tablespoons onion, finely chopped

⅛ teaspoon each salt and black pepper

2 cups frozen Southern-style hash browns, thawed

TIP: Try other soup flavors such as cream of chicken or nacho cheese. Use frozen O'Brien potatoes and party dip in place of hash browns and sour cream. Top casserole with other cheeses like cheddar, Monterey Jack, or Mexican blend.

vegetarian

INSTRUCTIONS

1. Coat a 2-quart slow cooker with cooking spray.

2. In a medium bowl, stir together the sour cream, soup, cheese, onion, salt, and black pepper.

3. Add the hash browns and toss to coat. Spoon mixture into prepared cooker.

4. Cover and cook on high for 1½ hours. Reduce heat to low and cook 1½ hours more. Serve and enjoy!

Mexican Egg "Bake"

> *Serves 2 to 3*

INGREDIENTS

¼ cup chopped onion

4 frozen precooked sausage patties, thawed

½ teaspoon minced garlic

½ cup bell pepper, diced

¾ cup Pepper Jack or Mexican cheese blend, shredded, plus more for topping

5 eggs, lightly beaten

2 to 3 tablespoons chopped green chiles (from a 4 oz. can)

½ teaspoon chili powder

Dash cayenne pepper

Salt and black pepper, to taste

Salsa, sour cream, fresh cilantro, and/or black olives, for serving

Breakfast Burritos

Build your own breakfast burritos when you scoop the cooked Mexican Egg "Bake" onto flour or whole wheat tortillas. Serve with red or green salsa, sour cream, and other toppings as desired.

INSTRUCTIONS

1. Coat a 1½-quart slow cooker with cooking spray.

2. Place the onion in cooker. Crumble the sausage over onion. Top evenly with the garlic, bell pepper, and ¾ cup cheese; set aside.

3. In a medium bowl, whisk together the eggs, chiles, chili powder, cayenne pepper, salt, and black pepper.

4. Pour the egg mixture over ingredients in cooker.

5. Cover and cook on low for 3 to 4 hours or until set and cooked through. Serve with salsa, sour cream, fresh cilantro, and black olives as desired.

Loaded Tater Tot "Bake"

> *Serves 2*

INGREDIENTS

2 to 2½ cups frozen mini tater tots, thawed

¼ pound Canadian bacon slices, halved

½ cup onion, chopped

¾ cup shredded cheddar cheese

2 tablespoons grated Parmesan cheese

3 eggs

¼ cup half-and-half

1 tablespoon flour

Salt and black pepper, to taste

Real bacon bits, for sprinkling

INSTRUCTIONS

1. Coat a 1½-quart slow cooker with cooking spray.

2. Place one-third of the tater tots in cooker, followed by one-third each of the Canadian bacon, onion, cheddar, and Parmesan. Repeat layers two more times; set aside.

3. In a small bowl, whisk together the eggs, half-and-half, and flour until smooth. Season with salt and black pepper. Pour evenly over layers in cooker and sprinkle bacon bits over the top.

4. Cover and cook on low about 4 hours or until cooked through. Serve and enjoy!

TIP: Change it up with different meats, such as sliced, pre-cooked sausage links, and other cheeses, or add chopped bell peppers and sliced mushrooms.

Cheesy Salsa Chicken

> *Serves 2*

INGREDIENTS

2 boneless, skinless chicken breast halves

1½ teaspoons taco seasoning

½ cup salsa

½ (10.7 ounce) can nacho cheese soup (about ½ cup)

¼ cup sour cream, plus more for serving

6 flour tortillas or tortilla chips, for serving

Lettuce, onions, tomatoes, and shredded cheddar cheese, for serving

INSTRUCTIONS

1. Place the chicken in a 1½-quart oval slow cooker. Sprinkle evenly with taco seasoning.

2. In a small bowl, stir together the salsa and soup; pour over chicken.

3. Cover and cook on low for 6 to 8 hours.

4. Remove the chicken from cooker and shred meat. Return shredded meat to cooker and stir in sour cream.

5. Serve on tortillas with lettuce, onion, tomatoes, shredded cheddar, and sour cream, or keep warm and serve as a hearty dip with tortilla chips.

Serve It Whole

After cooking, set each chicken breast half on a bed of rice (do not shred). Stir sour cream into sauce mixture and drizzle it on top. Sprinkle with shredded cheddar cheese. Enjoy!

Vegetarian Minestrone

❯ *Serves 2 to 3*

INGREDIENTS

1½ cups vegetable broth

⅔ cup tomatoes, diced

⅓ cup kidney beans, drained and rinsed

¼ cup onion, diced

¼ cup celery, diced

½ cup baby carrots, sliced

½ cup frozen green beans, thawed

½ teaspoon minced garlic

1 teaspoon fresh parsley, minced

¼ teaspoon black pepper

¼ teaspoon dried oregano

⅛ teaspoon black pepper

⅛ teaspoon dried thyme

½ cup cooked elbow macaroni

1 cup baby spinach, chopped

1 to 2 tablespoons shredded Romano cheese, for topping

vegetarian

INSTRUCTIONS

1. In a 2-quart slow cooker, combine the vegetable broth, tomatoes, kidney beans, onion, celery, carrots, green beans, garlic, parsley, salt, oregano, black pepper, and thyme. Stir well.

2. Cover and cook on low for 6 to 8 hours.

3. Approximately 15 minutes before serving, stir in the cooked macaroni and spinach; cover and cook on low until heated through (spinach wilts).

4. Divide among serving bowls and sprinkle with the Romano.

Slow-Cooked Roast Beef

Place a sliced onion and a 1- to- 1½-pound beef roast in a small slow cooker; season with salt and black pepper. Cover and cook on low for 8 to 10 hours. Shred the meat and add to this soup, or slice and serve as desired.

BBQ Ribs

❯ *Serves 2*

INGREDIENTS

1½ to 1¾ pounds pork baby
 back ribs

Salt and black pepper, to taste

½ cup ketchup

¼ cup chili sauce

½ cup onion, finely diced

2 tablespoons brown sugar

1 tablespoon distilled white vinegar

½ teaspoon dried oregano

½ teaspoon Worcestershire sauce

Dash of hot sauce

TIP: Prepare sauce as directed, but pour it over other meats in a slow cooker, such as chicken, ham, pork chops, or beef roast. Cook on low until tender and fully cooked.

INSTRUCTIONS

1. Cut the ribs into two equal slabs (about three ribs each) and arrange in a 1½-quart oval slow cooker.

2. Season with salt and black pepper. Cover and begin cooking on high.

3. Meanwhile, in a small bowl, mix the ketchup, chili sauce, onion, brown sugar, vinegar, oregano, Worcestershire sauce, and hot sauce. Pour sauce mixture over ribs and turn to coat well.

4. Cover and reduce heat to low; cook for 7 to 9 hours or until tender. Skim off accumulated grease.

5. Serve ribs with sauce. Enjoy!

Ham & Bean Soup

> *Serves 2*

INGREDIENTS

⅔ cup dried great northern beans (soaked overnight)

2 cups chicken broth

⅓ cup ham, diced

½ cup onion, chopped

¼ cup carrot, grated

¼ cup celery, chopped

2 tablespoons celery leaves, chopped

¼ teaspoon chili powder

1 bay leaf

Garlic salt and black pepper, to taste

INSTRUCTIONS

1. Drain and rinse soaked the beans.

2. In a 1½ quart slow cooker, combine beans, chicken broth, ham, onion, carrot, celery, celery leaves, chili powder, and bay leaf.

3. Cover and cook on low for 6 to 8 hours.

4. Discard the bay leaf and season with garlic salt and black pepper before serving.

To Soak Beans

Sort through dry beans, removing any damaged ones or small stones. Rinse beans in a colander. Transfer to a bowl, cover with fresh water, and let soak overnight (at least 8 hours). Remove any floating beans; drain and rinse before cooking.

Bacon-Apple Chicken

> *Serves 2*

INGREDIENTS

- 2 boneless, skinless chicken breast halves
- 4 bacon strips
- ½ cup BBQ sauce
- 2 tablespoons brown sugar
- 1 tablespoon lemon juice
- 1 large Gala apple, peeled and chopped

INSTRUCTIONS

1. Wrap each chicken breast half with two bacon strips and place side by side in a 1½-quart oval slow cooker.

2. In a small bowl, mix the BBQ sauce, brown sugar, lemon juice, and apple. Pour sauce mixture over chicken.

3. Cover and cook on low for 3½ to 5 hours or until chicken is cooked through. Serve and enjoy!

Shred It

Shred the cooked chicken and fill pita pockets or buns. Drizzle with some of the apple-barbecue sauce and serve with shredded cabbage or lettuce and condiments as desired.

Meatball Sliders

> *Serves 2*

INGREDIENTS

8 ounces (about 15 small) cooked frozen meatballs, thawed

½ cup tomato sauce

½ cup diced tomatoes with green chiles

¼ teaspoon garlic powder

2 teaspoons fresh parsley, chopped

5 slider buns

Provolone cheese, sliced

TIP: Serve meatballs and sauce over your favorite cooked pasta and sprinkle with freshly grated Romano or Parmesan cheese.

INSTRUCTIONS

1. Place the meatballs in a 2-quart slow cooker.

2. Pour the tomato sauce and tomatoes with juice over meatballs. Sprinkle evenly with garlic powder and parsley.

3. Cover and cook on high for 3 hours. Serve on buns with provolone and a little sauce.

Italian Potatoes

> *Serves 2 to 3*

INGREDIENTS

½ small onion, thinly sliced

2 large russet potatoes, peeled

½ small green bell pepper, sliced

Salt and black pepper, to taste

1 teaspoon Italian seasoning

⅔ cup spaghetti sauce

1 cup shredded Italian cheese blend, plus more for sprinkling

Grated Parmesan cheese

TIP: Add layers of sliced pepperoni (approximately 1½ ounce) and/or ½ pound browned, drained Italian sausage; slow cook as directed.

INSTRUCTIONS

1. Place half the onion in a 2-quart slow cooker.

2. Slice the potatoes into thin rounds. Layer half the potato slices over onions, followed by half the bell pepper slices.

3. Season with salt and black pepper; sprinkle with ½ teaspoon Italian seasoning.

4. Spread with half the spaghetti sauce and half the Italian cheese. Repeat layers.

5. Cover and cook on low for 3½ to 5 hours or until potatoes are tender.

6. Near end of cooking time, sprinkle additional Italian cheese and Parmesan on top; cover and cook 10 minutes more.

Shrimp Creole

> *Serves 2*

INGREDIENTS

¾ cup celery, diced

½ cup onion, chopped

⅓ cup bell pepper, diced

½ cup tomato sauce

1 (14.5 ounce) can diced tomatoes

½ teaspoon minced garlic

½ teaspoon Creole seasoning

¼ teaspoon salt

⅛ teaspoon black pepper

2 to 3 drops hot sauce

½ pound frozen cooked
    shrimp, thawed

Cooked brown or white rice or
    angel hair pasta, for serving

INSTRUCTIONS

1. In a 1½-quart slow cooker, combine the celery, onion, bell pepper, tomato sauce, tomatoes with juice, garlic, Creole seasoning, salt, black pepper, and hot sauce; stir well.

2. Cover and cook on high for 3 to 4 hours.

3. During the last 15 to 30 minutes of cooking time, stir in shrimp and reduce heat to low.

4. Cover and cook until the shrimp is just heated through. Serve over hot rice or pasta.

TIP: Before adding shrimp, sauce may be thickened with a mixture of 1½ teaspoons cornstarch dissolved in 1 tablespoon cold water. Stir into sauce, cover, and cook on high until thickened.

Beef Stroganoff

> *Serves 2 to 3*

INGREDIENTS

¾ pound beef stew meat, cut into 1-inch pieces

⅓ cup onion, chopped

1 (10.7 ounce) can golden mushroom soup

1 (4 ounce) can sliced mushrooms, drained

⅛ teaspoon black pepper

¼ teaspoon minced garlic

Dash Worcestershire sauce

½ cup sour cream

Cooked noodles, rice, or mashed potatoes, for serving

INSTRUCTIONS

1. In a 1½-quart slow cooker, stir together the beef, onion, soup, mushrooms, black pepper, garlic, and Worcestershire sauce.

2. Cover and cook on low for 6 to 7 hours or until the meat is very tender.

3. Just before serving, stir in the sour cream until well blended and creamy. Serve over hot noodles, rice, or mashed potatoes.

TIP: Not quite ready to eat? Turn your slow cooker to "keep warm" setting to hold the stroganoff a bit longer. However, don't stir in the sour cream until just before serving.

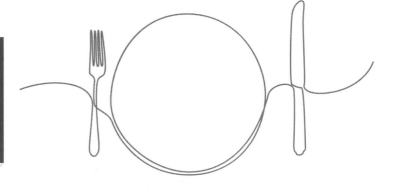

Stuffed Peppers

> *Serves 2*

INGREDIENTS

2 large bell peppers

⅔ cup frozen soy crumbles, thawed

¼ cup onion, finely chopped

½ teaspoon minced garlic

1 cup tomato sauce

¼ teaspoon each salt and
  ground cumin

⅛ teaspoon ground cinnamon

Dash each black and cayenne pepper

⅓ cup uncooked couscous

½ cup water

Shredded cheddar or Monterey Jack
  cheese, for serving

vegetarian

INSTRUCTIONS

1. Coat a 1½-quart oval slow cooker with cooking spray.

2. Cut off the stem end of each pepper and remove top, seeds, and membranes. Rinse and drain peppers.

3. In a medium bowl, combine the soy crumbles, onion, garlic, tomato sauce, salt, cumin, cinnamon, black pepper, and cayenne pepper; mix well. Stir in couscous.

4. Spoon half of mixture into each pepper. Pour the water into prepared cooker and set peppers upright inside.

5. Cover and cook on low for 4 to 6 hours or until peppers are tender. Sprinkle with cheese before serving.

Jerked Pulled Pork

> *Serves 2 to 3*

INGREDIENTS

½ teaspoon chili powder

¼ teaspoon ground allspice

⅛ teaspoon garlic powder

⅛ teaspoon salt

⅛ teaspoon black pepper

Dash ground nutmeg

Dash thyme

Dash cayenne pepper

2 tablespoons lime juice

1 (1 to 1¼ pound) pork tenderloin

1 small onion, sliced

1 cup BBQ sauce

2 tablespoons dark rum

4 large hamburger buns, for serving

TIP: For sliced pork, shorten cooking time to approximately 6 hours. Slice the meat, drizzle with sauce and onions, and serve with Hash Brown Casserole (recipe on page 128).

INSTRUCTIONS

1. In a small bowl, combine the chili powder, allspice, garlic powder, salt, black pepper, nutmeg, thyme, and cayenne pepper. Drizzle lime juice over tenderloin and then rub spice mixture into the meat.

2. Place meat in a zippered plastic bag; seal and refrigerate at least 3 hours or overnight to marinate.

3. To cook, place the onion in a 1½-quart slow cooker.

4. Remove tenderloin from marinade and cut into two or three even chunks. Set meat on onions in cooker.

5. In a small bowl, whisk together the BBQ sauce and rum; pour over meat.

6. Cover and cook on low for 8 to 10 hours or until meat is tender.

7. Remove the pork from cooker and shred the meat. Return shredded meat to cooker and stir until coated; cook until heated through, about 15 minutes.

8. Serve the meat and onions on buns with additional sauce on the side, if desired.

Black-Bean Tortilla Soup

> *Serves 2 to 3*

INGREDIENTS

1 cup black beans, drained and rinsed

1 cup chicken stock or broth

½ cup salsa

½ cup frozen whole kernel corn, thawed

Dash hot sauce

½ teaspoon minced garlic

½ teaspoon dried oregano

⅛ teaspoon ground cumin

¾ cup cooked, shredded chicken

1 teaspoon lime juice

½ cup shredded cheddar cheese

1 tablespoon green onion, chopped

Sour cream and tortilla strips, for topping

INSTRUCTIONS

1. In a 1½-quart slow cooker, stir together the beans, chicken stock, salsa, corn, hot sauce, garlic, oregano, and cumin.

2. Cover and cook on high for 2½ to 3½ hours.

3. Before serving, stir in the chicken and lime juice; cover and cook on high until heated through, about 20 minutes.

4. Divide among serving bowls and sprinkle with the cheese and green onion. Top with sour cream and a few tortilla strips.

Asian Orange Chicken

> *Serves 2*

INGREDIENTS

¼ cup onion, finely chopped

2 boneless, skinless chicken breast
    halves, cut into strips

½ bell pepper, cut into strips

3 tablespoons orange juice

½ teaspoon orange zest

1 teaspoon brown sugar

1 to 2 teaspoons candied ginger,
    finely sliced

½ cup orange marmalade

1 teaspoon soy sauce

2 tablespoons BBQ sauce

Dash garlic powder

Cooked rice or couscous,
    for serving

INSTRUCTIONS

1. In a 2-quart slow cooker, layer half the onion, half the chicken, and half the bell pepper strips; repeat layers.

2. In a small bowl, mix the orange juice, orange zest, and brown sugar; pour over chicken. Sprinkle ginger on top.

3. Cover and cook on high for 3 hours or until the chicken is almost cooked through.

4. Drain juices from slow cooker and reduce heat to low. In a small bowl, stir together the marmalade, soy sauce, barbecue sauce, and garlic powder; pour over chicken.

5. Cover and cook 30 minutes more or until the chicken is done. Serve over hot rice or couscous.

Slow Cooker Rice

In a buttered 1½-quart slow cooker, mix 1 cup rice, ¼ teaspoon salt, and scant 2 cups water. Cover and cook on high about 2 hours, stirring once. Reduce heat to warm, line lid with a paper towel to absorb moisture, and let rest 30 to 60 minutes. Fluff with a fork before serving.

Pizza Pasta Casserole

> *Serves 2 to 4*

INGREDIENTS

1½ cups uncooked spiral pasta

¼ pounds very lean ground beef

1¼ cup onion, chopped

¼ cup red bell pepper, chopped

½ teaspoon minced garlic

⅓ cup pepperoni, sliced
   and quartered

¼ cup black or green olives, sliced

¾ cup shredded mozzarella or pizza
   cheese blend, divided

1 cup pizza sauce

¼ cup water

Grated Parmesan cheese, for serving

INSTRUCTIONS

1. Coat a 1½-quart slow cooker with cooking spray.

2. Rinse the pasta in hot water and place in cooker.

3. Crumble the uncooked ground beef into cooker. Add the onion, bell pepper, garlic, pepperoni, olives, and ¼ cup mozzarella; stir to combine and set aside.

4. In a small bowl, mix the pizza sauce and water. Pour the sauce over mixture in cooker and stir well.

5. Cover and cook on low for 3½ to 4 hours or until the pasta is tender.

6. Toward end of cooking time, sprinkle with remaining ½ cup mozzarella; cover and let melt. Sprinkle with Parmesan just before serving.

Add Rice Instead!

In the slow cooker, combine 1 cup uncooked rice, 1½ cups pizza sauce, and 1¼ cups water. Stir in mushrooms, olives, onion, bell pepper, and pepperoni as desired. Cover and cook as directed above or until liquid is absorbed and rice is tender. Stir once and sprinkle with mozzarella; let melt before serving.

Pepper Steak

> *Serves 2 to 3*

INGREDIENTS

¼ cup flour

½ teaspoon garlic powder

¾ pound beef sirloin steak, sliced into strips

½ medium onion, thinly sliced

1½ teaspoons soy sauce

1½ teaspoons sesame oil or vegetable oil

½ teaspoon brown sugar

3 tablespoons tomato sauce

½ teaspoon beef bouillon granules, dissolved in 1 tablespoon hot water

½ each green and red bell pepper, sliced or chunked

Cooked rice or mashed potatoes, for serving

INSTRUCTIONS

1. In a large, zippered plastic bag, mix the flour and garlic powder. Add the beef strips and seal bag; shake until meat is evenly coated.

2. Place the onion and meat in a 1½-quart slow cooker.

3. In a small bowl, mix the soy sauce, oil, brown sugar, tomato sauce, and bouillon water. Pour over the meat in cooker and stir to combine.

4. Cover and cook on low for 5 to 7 hours.

5. During the last 1 to 2 hours of cooking time, stir in the bell peppers and continue to cook until the meat is tender and peppers reach desired doneness.

6. Serve over hot rice or mashed potatoes.

TIP: Purchase pre-sliced stir-fry beef or ask your grocer to slice the steak into strips for you.

BBQ Pork Chops

> *Serves 2*

INGREDIENTS

2 (1-inch thick) boneless loin pork chops*

½ small onion, sliced

¼ teaspoon garlic powder

½ cup BBQ sauce

2 teaspoons cornstarch (optional)

> *If chops have been "butterflied," fold in half before placing in cooker.*

INSTRUCTIONS

1. Trim excess fat from the pork chops.

2. Place most of the onion slices in a 1½-quart oval slow cooker and set chops on top, side by side.

3. Arrange the remaining onion slices over chops and sprinkle with garlic powder; pour BBQ sauce on top.

4. Cover and cook on low for 4 to 5 hours or until meat is cooked through.

5. Remove the chops to a serving platter and keep warm. If desired, thicken sauce by dissolving cornstarch in 1 tablespoon water; stir into sauce from cooker and microwave on high for 1 to 2 minutes until thickened, stirring once.

6. Serve sauce with pork chops.

Delicious Duo:

Pair this with BBQ Pork Chops!

Garlic Smashed Potatoes

> *Serves 2*

INGREDIENTS

3½ cups red potatoes, diced
3 teaspoons minced garlic
1 cup chicken broth
2 tablespoons butter
2 ounces cream cheese
3 to 5 tablespoons half-and-half

INSTRUCTIONS

1. In a 2-quart slow cooker, combine the potatoes, garlic, and chicken broth.

2. Cover and cook on high for 3 to 4 hours.

3. Drain the potatoes, reserving liquid.

4. Add the butter, cream cheese, and half-and-half to potatoes and mash well, adding reserved liquid as needed. Season and keep warm until serving.

Cheesy Potatoes & Ham

> *Serves 2 to 3*

INGREDIENTS

1½ cups frozen O'Brien
   potatoes, thawed

1 cup cooked ham, diced

1 cup shredded cheddar cheese

1 cup frozen cut green
   beans, thawed

1 (10.7 ounce) can cream of
   potato soup

Dash onion powder

¼ cup carrot, shredded (optional)

¼ cup sour cream

Fresh chives, chopped, to taste

½ cup French-fried onions

INSTRUCTIONS

1. Coat a 1½-quart slow cooker with cooking spray. In cooker, stir together the potatoes, ham, cheddar, green beans, soup, onion powder, and carrot, if desired.

2. Cover and cook on low for 5 to 6 hours.

3. Toward end of cooking time, stir in the sour cream and chives. Sprinkle the fried onions over the top.

4. Cover and cook 5 minutes more or until the onions are just heated through. Serve and enjoy!

TIP: Purchase the ham, cheese, and carrots already diced or shredded. Substitute the onion powder and fresh chives by using chive and onion-flavored sour cream.

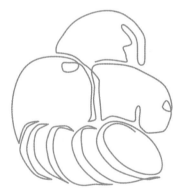

Glazed Sweet Potatoes

> *Serves 2*

vegetarian

INGREDIENTS

½ cup orange juice

1 tablespoon cornstarch

2 tablespoons butter, melted

Dash salt

⅓ cup brown sugar

1 (15 ounce) can sweet
    potatoes, drained

INSTRUCTIONS

1. In a 1½-quart slow cooker, mix the orange juice and cornstarch until dissolved.

2. Stir in the butter, salt, and brown sugar. Add sweet potatoes and toss to coat.

3. Cover and cook on high for 3 hours.

4. Turn off heat, stir gently, and let rest at least 10 minutes to allow the glaze to thicken. Serve and enjoy!

For a Sweeter Sauce

Peel and slice 2 or 3 medium sweet potatoes and place in a buttered 1½- to 2-quart slow cooker. Prepare glaze mixture as directed, substitute apple cider for the orange juice pour over potatoes and toss lightly. Cover and cook on low for 5 to 7 hours.

S'mores Brownies

> *Serves 2 to 3*

INGREDIENTS

2½ tablespoons butter

2 tablespoons plus ½ cup mini milk chocolate chips, divided

1 egg

¼ cup sugar

½ teaspoon vanilla extract

3 tablespoons flour

1½ teaspoons unsweetened cocoa powder

Dash salt

3 or 4 graham cracker squares

¾ cup mini marshmallows

TIP: Brownies may look undercooked in the center even when done. If brownies buckle when foil is lifted, cook longer and check every 15 minutes until firm enough to remove.

vegetarian

INSTRUCTIONS

1. Line a 1½-quart slow cooker with foil and coat with cooking spray.

2. Melt the butter and 2 tablespoons chocolate chips together; stir and let cool.

3. In a medium bowl, beat together the egg, sugar, and vanilla; whisk in melted chocolate. Stir in the flour, cocoa powder, and salt until blended. Pour half of the batter into prepared cooker.

4. Cover the batter with a layer of graham cracker squares, breaking and piecing together as needed.

5. Sprinkle remaining ½ cup chocolate chips over crackers and top with remaining batter.

6. Cover and cook on low for 3 to 4 hours or until firm. Remove the brownies from cooker by lifting foil; let cool on foil.

7. Before serving, sprinkle the marshmallows over brownies. Set foil with brownies under broiler for 30 to 60 seconds or until marshmallows are toasted. Watch closely to avoid burning. Cool slightly before cutting. Serve and enjoy!

Stuffed Apple Duo

> *Serves 2*

vegetarian

INGREDIENTS

¼ cup brown sugar

2 tablespoons dried sweetened cranberries or raisins

2 tablespoons pecans, chopped

1 teaspoon ground cinnamon

⅛ teaspoon ground allspice

Dash salt

2 large apples, your choice (I used Pink Lady)

2 tablespoons butter

½ cup cranberry-apple juice or water

Ice cream or whipped topping

INSTRUCTIONS

1. In a small bowl, stir together the brown sugar, cranberries, pecans, cinnamon, allspice, and salt; set aside.

2. With a knife or melon baller, cut out each apple's stem and core, leaving bottoms of apples intact to hold fillings. Enlarge holes near the top and peel off a narrow strip of apple skin around openings.

3. Stuff each apple with half the brown sugar mixture, poking it down firmly to make room for more filling. Top each apple with 1 tablespoon butter.

4. Pour the juice into a 1½-quart oval slow cooker and set stuffed apples upright inside.

5. Cover and cook on low for 6 to 7 hours or until fork tender.

6. To serve, drizzle apples with the remaining sauce from cooker and serve warm with ice cream or whipped topping, if desired.

For Caramel Lovers

Try stuffing each apple with 2 tablespoons brown sugar, 3 cinnamon red-hot candies, 1 tablespoon butter, and 1 or 2 unwrapped caramels. Sprinkle lightly with cinnamon and cook with apple juice until tender.

Caramel-Rum Fondue

> *Serves 2 to 3*

INGREDIENTS

1 (14 ounce) package caramels, unwrapped

⅔ cup heavy cream

½ cup mini marshmallows

1 tablespoon rum (or ½ teaspoon rum extract)

Assorted dippers (apple wedges, strawberries, donut holes, cubes of cereal-marshmallow treats, gingersnaps, vanilla wafers, Nutter Butters, shortbread cookies, etc.)

Waffle bowls, optional

INSTRUCTIONS

1. Lightly coat a 1½-quart slow cooker with cooking spray. Place the caramels and cream in cooker.

2. Cover and cook on low for 1½ to 2 hours or until melted, stirring occasionally.

3. Stir in the marshmallows and rum. Cover and continue cooking on low (or warm setting) 20 to 30 minutes more.

4. Keep warm and serve with assorted dippers in edible waffle bowls, if desired.

TIP: For more fun, dip caramel-coated foods into scrumptious toppings like coconut, chopped peanuts, chopped raisins, toffee bits, mini chocolate chips, or chopped M&Ms.

Blueberry Cobbler

> *Serves 2 to 3*

INGREDIENTS

¼ cup plus 1 tablespoon flour, divided

2 tablespoons plus ¼ cup sugar, divided

¼ teaspoon baking powder

Salt, to taste

Pinch each of ground cinnamon and ground nutmeg

1 egg

1½ teaspoons milk

1½ teaspoons vegetable oil

1 cup fresh or frozen blueberries, thawed

3 tablespoons brown sugar

¼ cup quick oats

1½ tablespoons butter

2 tablespoons pecans, chopped

TIP: Use fresh seasonal berries, such as raspberries, blackberries, or a combination of your favorites. Serve with frozen yogurt, ice cream, or whipped cream.

vegetarian

INSTRUCTIONS

1. Coat a 1½-quart slow cooker with cooking spray.

2. In a small bowl, combine ¼ cup flour, 2 tablespoons sugar, baking powder, a dash of salt, cinnamon, and nutmeg; set aside.

3. In another bowl, whisk together the egg, milk, and oil; add to flour mixture and stir until moistened. Spread batter in prepared cooker.

4. In a medium bowl, combine remaining 1 tablespoon flour, remaining ¼ cup sugar, and dash of salt. Add the blueberries and stir until coated; scatter evenly over batter in cooker.

5. Cover and cook on high for 1½ to 2 hours or until cobbler tests done with a toothpick.

6. Meanwhile, mix the brown sugar and oats. Cut in the butter until crumbly; stir in pecans. Sprinkle the mixture over cobbler; cover and cook on high 15 to 20 minutes more.

7. Uncover and let rest 10 minutes before serving.

Orange Cheesecake

> *Serves 2*

INGREDIENTS

6 tablespoons chocolate wafer cookie crumbs

4 tablespoons sugar, divided

1½ tablespoons butter, melted

5 ounces cream cheese, softened

1 egg

1 tablespoon frozen orange juice concentrate

¼ teaspoon orange flavoring

½ teaspoon orange zest, plus more for garnishing

1½ teaspoons flour

¼ teaspoon vanilla extract

Fudge ice cream topping, for drizzling

TIP: Instead of a chocolate crust, make it with graham cracker or vanilla wafer crumbs. Before serving, top cheesecake with whipped cream, orange zest, and mandarin oranges.

INSTRUCTIONS

1. Place one or two metal canning jar rings in the bottom of a 1½-quart slow cooker to act as a riser during cooking. Set a 4-inch springform pan on top to check fit; remove pan and set aside.

2. In a small bowl, mix the crumbs, 1 tablespoon sugar, and butter. Pat into bottom and partway up sides of springform pan; set aside.

3. In another bowl, beat together the cream cheese and remaining 3 tablespoons sugar until creamy. Add egg and beat for 3 minutes.

4. Add the juice concentrate, orange flavoring, ½ teaspoon orange zest, flour, and vanilla; beat 2 more minutes. Pour mixture into crust and set pan on riser in cooker.

5. Cover and cook on high for 2 to 2½ hours or until firm around edges (center should still jiggle slightly when pan is lightly shaken).

6. Turn off heat and let rest for 1 hour or until pan is cool enough to remove.

7. Cool completely before removing sides of pan. Chill.

8. Before serving, drizzle with fudge topping and garnish with more orange zest.

Index

Note: Page numbers followed by another *page number in parentheses--e.g.,89 (*104-5)--indicates Delicious Duo paired recipes.